# PLEASURE

EMMA-LOUISE BOYNTON

# PLEASURE

## The reclamation of my body

LEAP

First published in the UK in 2026 by LEAP
An imprint of Bonnier Books UK
5th Floor, HYLO, 105 Bunhill Row,
London, EC1Y 8LZ



A CIP catalogue record for this book is available from the British Library.

Hardback ISBN: 9781785129711
Trade Paperback ISBN: 9781785125041

*Also available as an ebook and an audiobook*

1 3 5 7 9 10 8 6 4 2

Design and Typeset by Envy Design Ltd.
Printed and bound in Great Britain by CPI (UK) Ltd, Croydon CR0 4YY

The authorised representative in the EEA is Bonnier Books UK (Ireland) Limited.
Registered office address:
Block B, The Crescent Building
Northwood, Santry
Dublin 9, D09 C6X8
Ireland
compliance@bonnierbooks.ie

www.bonnierbooks.co.uk

*To Adriaane, Graham and Lucy.*
*My forever loves.*

# Contents

# Author's Note

Throughout this book, when I use the term 'women' I intend for it to mean *all women*, very much including our trans sisters. While the experiences reflected here speak mostly to my own experiences as a cis woman, I hope that the thoughts explored may still, at least in part, be of value to women with different experiences to my own.

# The Cool Girl and the Sex Addict

He picked me up in his four-by-four, which looked bloated and oversized, humming away on the narrow street as I ran around my bedroom shoving things into a giant bag. I had that heavy sense of foreboding which always precedes a break-up.

'You carry your possessions like armour,' a therapist once told me, 'a mechanism through which you try to impose control over your day, a way of dealing with the anxiety of worldly uncertainty by always being over-prepared with *stuff*.' Perhaps she was right, I thought, as I shoved two cardigans and an extra scarf into a tote, as though this wad of wool might quell my mounting anxiety. A 'recovered' anorexic has to get their control fix somehow.

We'd planned to drive to the countryside today, somewhere far away where we could walk and talk for hours.

But as I got into the car, he said he'd changed his mind. There wasn't time – he now had to be back before lunch and, besides, it was a grey and overcast day. I nodded in agreement as he suggested we go somewhere closer, thinking this was exactly why our non-relationship had to end. Because not a single plan nor promise was ever adhered to. And because he is a sex addict and I'm fuelling his addiction.

As he drove me home from our half-hearted ramble in a field somewhere off the A1, I grew teary. The situation felt like it demanded it. I felt I owed the whole affair some sort of final performance, as much for myself as for him. This is what dating was supposed to look and feel like, I told myself. He pulled over to the side of the road and kissed me. A goodbye sort of kiss that turned into a snog and then suddenly he was pulling his dick out of his trousers, as he so often did, telling me for the umpteenth time just how hard I made him. In the near distance, kids shouted as they kicked a ball across the grass, their parents clapping loudly in support.

'Someone will see,' I told him, throwing my scarf over his lap as he moved his hand up and down. I kissed him again awkwardly and he moved his hand faster, biting my lip as his eyes clouded over with the determined stare of the deeply aroused. Finally, he let out a satisfied moan before slumping back into his seat, a smile dancing across his wet lips. I rolled my eyes and grabbed the scarf from his lap, a warm patch of damp spread across the area in which he'd come. He restarted the engine, and we returned to the road.

'If you ever want to have casual, consequence-less sex with someone,' he said, eyes fixed on the license plate in front of him, 'anytime, any day – just call me.' I nodded, wondering if sex for me could ever be so devoid of feeling as to be fully without consequence. Ten minutes later, we were back outside my flat. With my come-soaked scarf bundled into my bag, I said a final goodbye and got out of the car.

We had started having sex some three or so months earlier. A novelty to me because I had only recently finished seeing a sex therapist and was in the early throes of trying to figure out what kind of relationship to intimacy I now wanted to establish. Or rather, what kind of sex did I actually like? These were questions that had long evaded me, since I'd moved through my twenties convinced I was broken. I didn't enjoy sex in the way everyone around me seemed to, and I couldn't orgasm with the frequency or ease with which my friends appeared accustomed. Truthfully, I couldn't orgasm at all.

But I feigned nonchalance in this area of my life, relishing occasional flings for their quick hit of intimacy, while dreading actually having sex. It's not that I didn't like it per se, or not always, but more that my body's perceived inability to function as expected felt like a blight on my personhood – on my womanhood. Like every Good Girl or Woman, I had perfected the performance of pleasure with aplomb. I knew how to writhe and moan and move my body to a sexual rhythm; I'd just lost, or perhaps never truly discovered, the ability to enjoy it.

And so while my body performed pleasure, my mind wandered off. I thought about what else I might be doing, where else I could be. I worried about what I looked like and how I was being perceived. I wondered how long it would take for the other person to realise I was only ever half there, staring somewhere into the distance as I waited for it to be over.

We are quick to attribute this sort of mind-versus-body dualism to French philosopher Rene Descartes, whose writing in the early 17th century spawned his now-notorious philosophical soundbite: 'I think, therefore I am' (*Cogito, ergo sum*). This framework became foundational in Western philosophy and medicine, underpinning the notion that rational thought is superior to sensation, and that the body is something to be overcome or controlled. Following an adolescence trapped in the firm grasp of an eating disorder, this is precisely how I looked upon my own flesh: as an out-of-control monster in constant need of containment. The deprivation of nourishment was my disciplinary tool.

But Descartes never made so clear and binary a distinction as is often suggested. He insisted they were separate substances, yes, but also 'intimately joined and intermingled', bound together in ways he could never fully explain. And as Western thought has slowly arrived at the realisation that the body is not an object we can live in opposition to, but the very ground of experience, the place where memory, trauma and pleasure register, I too had eventually to recognise the impossibility of living in opposition to this body I now call home.

This return of sorts could not have happened had I not finally decided, at age 28, to start sex therapy. To finally address my not being able to climax as a byproduct of disconnection as opposed to an irredeemable personal flaw. So where memoirist Melissa Febos writes in her latest book *The Dry Season* about finding respite from her dependence on love in celibacy, a practice that opened up her life 'like a mansion, half of whose rooms had been locked', my own palatial homecoming started the moment I repaired my relationship to pleasure and began, for the first time, to enjoy sex.

But perhaps Febos and I aren't so very different here. For we each had to revisit the stories that had shaped how we connected to intimacy – some different, some very much the same. And we both had to figure out what mythology we'd been handed that had profoundly shaped how we saw our bodies and who they were for. And what needed to be discarded in order that we could live in some sort of harmony with our own desires – desires formed in the crucible of patriarchy and shaped all too often in service, solely, of men.

Now, I needed to lean into the space of my sexuality for what felt like the first time and interrogate what had created such a profound chasm between my mind and my body. I had to let go, at least to begin with, of the propulsion to have sex *for* men so that I could find my way back to myself. And so that I could eventually come . . . again. It was an idea implanted in me one evening at a dinner party, when a woman turned to me and said, 'You know you can change that – your relationship to sex, I mean.'

It was late November, and the air outside was heavy with the lingering smoke of a bonfire. The dinner party host had just refilled my glass of wine and was beginning to hand around a large tiramisu, spooning delicious-looking dollops of fresh clotted cream into small dishes. I hadn't had an evening like this in some time – in the company of a group of near-strangers, drinking and chatting into the night. The UK had recently been subject to a succession of punitive lockdowns, and after years of uncertainty as to when life would return to some semblance of normality, I had grown wearily accustomed to a much smaller sort of life. It felt good to be out. To be speaking to unfamiliar faces where I was used to seeing only my own pixelated flesh in a little box at the corner of a Zoom screen. How long this temporary release would last, I didn't know, but I'd relish it for as long as it did.

'You need to go and see Aleks,' the woman to my left continued, tapping the end of her cigarette into an ashtray. 'She changed my relationship to sex entirely, and Holly's.'

I didn't know anyone sitting at that table, bar the host, which might be why I felt somewhat liberated to talk about a topic I seldom wanted to touch: sex. Under the veil of anonymity offered by the company of strangers, I had started to explain to my fellow dinner party guests the nuances of my somewhat complicated relationship to intimacy. Yes, the pandemic had warped things, and no, I didn't have any diagnosable condition, but unlike my pudding-consuming companions, I could not consider myself a *sexual* person. When I said I hadn't been able to orgasm since my first and only Great Break-Up some five or so years ago, both women looked horrified. I'd never relayed this piece of wholly un-salacious gossip to anyone before, so I was taken aback by their reaction. I thought people were either sexual or not, and that I was in the latter camp and there was nothing to be done about it.

As it transpired, both women had also struggled with their relationship to sex, but rather than admitting defeat like me, they'd taken the more decisive action of going to see a sex therapist – an Australian-based woman called Aleks Trkulja. They'd since become evangelicals for the sex therapy cause. Little did I know, I would eventually join them, becoming the most zealous of the proselytisers.

## Sex as performance

In 2021, an article entitled 'Everyone's Beautiful and No One's Horny'[1] went viral. It argued that as a society we've become increasingly obsessed with looking good, turning the body into a project we must constantly optimise in pursuit of ever more unrealistic aesthetic goals. Taking aim at the film industry, it noted how the people we see on our screens have become almost godlike in appearance, with rippling abs, bulging muscles and enviable complexions. Since the pursuit of beauty is no longer something to hide, but is itself deemed worthy of celebration, the gruelling exercise regimes it takes to achieve these exalted, Herculean proportions are now baked into promo tours. A visual feast upon which we're invited to gorge. And yet, these hyper-beautiful bodies have, it said, been stripped of their sex appeal, reduced to aesthetic spectacles devoid of desire or emotion. Bodies are hot, but no one is horny, revealing a cultural puritanism that reflects a wider flattening of sexuality. We admire bodies, but we're discouraged from acknowledging or expressing real sexual desire in all its human, fleshy messiness.

What the article captured was larger than the pandemic-induced sexual deprivation many of us were feeling at the time. It articulated how our increasingly visual, technologised culture has become so disembodied that it is, paradoxically, de-eroticised. And this is happening even as sex saturates our cultural landscape more overtly than ever. Not, as the writer suggested, because sex has disappeared – there may be less sex in films, but there's more sexualised imagery across the rest of our visual culture – but because sex has been displaced into performance.

I recently revisited the article as I began researching the topic of pleasure. It resonated more several years on – now that I understood my own experience of sexual alienation through the lens of performance stripped of sensation. I could situate my pre-sex therapy self in the de-eroticised cultural landscape the author described. Neither hot nor horny, just inexplicably frightened of my little-explored, or understood, desires. While I started sex therapy thinking I was disconnected from my body thanks to our taboo-laden sex culture, which meant I never thought to discuss, let alone try to fix, the finer details of my intimate life, I quickly realised it wasn't just this silence that separated me from myself. It was the idea that my body, my pleasure, was something to be performed rather than enjoyed. That it was something to offer up for someone else's consumption rather than experience for myself.

In his 1975 sort-of memoir, *The Philosophy of Andy Warhol (From A to B and Back Again)*, Andy Warhol wrote that 'sex is more exciting on the screen and between the pages than between the sheets.' His rationale: in the chasm that lies between fantasy and reality, fantasy, was always better. In fact, it was the root of desire, and was in many ways spoiled by the real thing. Even when we're having sex, he said, the enjoyment comes in part from a nostalgia for when you *used* to want it – 'sex is nostalgia for sex.' The sentiment feels truer than ever in today's technologised age in which we are all so chronically online: experiencing the event through our phones or else capturing it for online consumption. British adults now spend up to seven hours and 27 minutes a day on screens across different devices (smartphones, TVs, laptops, tablets, games consoles), with those aged 15–24 now spending almost five hours daily on their mobile phones specifically[2]. Globally, average screen time is around six to seven hours per day[3]. That means we're spending up to 30% of each day experiencing life through a digital peephole, as opposed to being truly present in our bodies. Social media has turned experience into nostalgia for experience.

Warhol might have been pleased to see just how saturated

in the sexual simulacrum popular culture is today. From TV shows to social media, newspapers to Substacks, porn to OnlyFans, the representation of sex abounds. And in ever-more titillating ways as content is reduced to clickbait to attract increasingly distracted eyeballs. But against the landscape of a sexualised media culture that continues to entertain and shock is a reported drop in the amount of sex people are actually having, and a decline in the number of relationships being formed. That's according to large-scale studies from across the UK, US, Europe and East Asia over the past decade – most notably since the late 2010s. According to the UK's NATSAL survey (the world's largest sex survey), reported sexual frequency in Britain has declined across successive studies since their research began in the early 1990s.[4] All while *Rolling Stone* declared sex parties mainstream in 2022. (Interestingly, Tim Berners-Lee, the inventor of the World Wide Web, supposedly commented: 'Legend has it that every new technology is first used for something related to sex or pornography.' I find it amusing to imagine that we live in a phone-addled world because people were desperate for a more convenient wank.)

But it's not just that we're physically spending more time on our phones and thus less time exploring and connecting to our bodies. In today's visual society, in which we're fixated on the aesthetic, sex (as it's served to us on screen) has been reduced to a disembodied experience. Something packaged up like one of Warhol's tin can prints: as entertainment; as something to consume rather than do; to watch rather than feel. This is the antithesis of what writer Audre Lorde described when she spoke of the erotic as something felt deep within us, a wellspring of creativity and joy that transcends the mere performance of sex disconnected from feeling.

And it's not just because porn is more instantly accessible, although it is. Porn has blended into mainstream media in a way that further normalises sex as performance, often in service of the male gaze. Sites like OnlyFans don't have an explore page, so porn creators have to build and leverage their following across other social platforms in order to establish an audience and drive revenue. Those who make the most online are the ones who understand the algorithm – who can capture people's attention, turn attention into audience, and audience into paying subscribers. People like Fansly star Bonnie Blue have honed this craft to perfection. From her headline-grabbing sex stunts to her purposefully provocative social content, she keeps us glued to her show – on her own channels and across mainstream media, which remains as fascinated by her as the thousands of men with whom she has sex. They queue up for hours! In masks! Even in the cold! Bonnie has redefined sex as spectacle for the digital age. Broadcasting daily a depiction, or at least an insinuation, of sex in pursuit of profit over pleasure. Sex work isn't new, but its seamless integration into our personal feeds is, collapsing the distinction between performance and the everyday. Add to this the rise of a wellness culture that treats sex as another site of optimisation, and the disembodiment intensifies.

I recently came across an article titled 'How To Biohack Your Sex Life',[5] which discussed the emerging spate of 'intelligent tools' being founded by biohacking experts 'to target our mental state and other aspects of our physiology', all in the name of 'deepening intimate connections and exploring the longevity of libido in an ageing population'. Among the experts highlighted was award-winning wellness 'visionary' and nutritionist Naomi Whittel, who claims women need to have 200 orgasms per year to maintain optimal health. That's roughly one orgasm every two days.

Wittel made this recommendation while speaking on the so-called 'father of biohacking' Dave Asprey's heroically titled podcast *Bulletproof Radio*, which focuses on biohacking, human performance and longevity. Orgasms, she said, not only help to boost our hormones and our mood, they are also excellent stress-busters. The advice follows a growing trend of health experts extolling the benefits of sex and orgasm as part of a wider project of self-optimisation.

According to Bryan Johnson, the Silicon Valley tech millionaire spending \$2 million per year to try and cheat death, 'you're 70% more likely to die prematurely if you're not having nighttime boners' (this is not backed up by science).[6] But don't be fooled into thinking he's prioritising sex and connection in his 'Blueprint', the comprehensive, data-driven anti-aging regimen by which he lives. No, instead he's hooking his penis up to a small device each night in order to monitor his erections while he sleeps. Then he compares his own erection data with that of his 19-year-old son's. In a blog post titled 'How I'm de-aging my penis',[7] he said he also measures his penis health through semen analysis; penile blood flow and a questionnaire to score sexual function, among other things. Does all of this enhance his sexual pleasure? It's unclear. But his rigid schedule and stringent dating rules – dinner at 11am; bedtime at 8:30pm; no pillow talk; no small talk; must give plasma – make dating challenging, he admits. It's hard to optimise intimacy.

Within this 'sex as self-improvement' discourse, sex is not about pleasure for the sake of pleasure, but rather the myriad life-extending health benefits it can potentially deliver. However valuable sexual health may be, reducing it to a data point turns the body into a system to be managed rather than something to be enjoyed. It's an approach devoid of intimacy or any meaningful connection to one's body.

So while the representation of sex is more culturally pervasive than ever, the model of sex being reinforced is disembodied and disconnected. It is fantasy over reality.

I often wonder what it would have been like to be introduced to my body as something worthy of exploring, pleasure a primary channel for discovery, as opposed to something I was supposed, somehow, to disavow – or else offer up in service of someone else's needs. Because sex is never just about sex, nor simply nostalgia. Sex is about being present in our bodies in a world that is constantly pulling us out of them. Sex is one way in which we connect to ourselves, push up against the limits of our physical experience, learn about our needs and explore our desires. When our cultural discourse flattens sex into spectacle or a tool for self-improvement, it deprives us of a model not just of intimacy, but of sensuality. Ultimately, it robs us of pleasure. It takes from us the sort of embodied self-ownership that is the real cornerstone of self-empowerment.

But I didn't know any of this when I booked my first sex therapy session with Aleks. I was fixated on the problem of my orgasm, or lack thereof. And I saw my body as a tool in service of a never-ending list of goals – something to be punished rather than enjoyed in my pursuit of their achievement. And I saw sex as something I did in order to please whoever I was sleeping with without ever considering my own desires. Namely, because I didn't know what they were.

I started sex therapy certain only of the fact that I felt broken and wanted to be fixed. In the end, it set me on a pathway to addressing three things. Firstly, how we reconnect to our bodies in a culture that has long separated women from themselves, couching our desires in shame and rendering our sexuality a source of fear and punishment rather than joy. Second, the power and necessity of weeding out whatever damaging sex myths have misshaped the way we see sex and our bodies. Then the importance of replacing these shame-laden stories with better ones. With stories about the power and importance of being connected to our bodies; about the pleasure these bodies can offer us if only we can move from performance to experience, from shame to connection. And finally, the transformative effect of getting to know yourself sexually. Because building confidence in the way we navigate our intimate lives has a ripple effect on everything else. You walk through the world differently when you're at peace with your body and connected to your pleasure.

Connecting to my sexuality was my route back to my own body and my introduction to real pleasure. And it all started in the therapy room.

*Chapter 1*

# 'The Door on the Female Mouth'

I sat on my bed with a hot water bottle tucked between my legs and the duvet cover pulled up to my waist. It was cold, but I was covered in a light sheen of sweat from nerves. I could feel my heart racing. I balanced my laptop on a cushion in front of me and got out a notebook and pen from my bedside drawer, ready to take notes should the urge arise. While my flatmate, Elspeth, sat in the room next door watching *The Real Housewives of Beverly Hills*, I readied myself to offer up the not-so-sordid details of my not-so-sordid sex life to a woman I had never met before. I suspected the level of detail into which we were about to delve would make me regret the whole thing instantly. But 'we can do hard things', I reminded myself, repeating Glennon Doyle's motivational affirmation as I waited for the purveyor of all sex wisdom to join me on Zoom.

Aleks's face suddenly filled the screen. My new sex therapist was sitting in a brightly lit living room, the sun pouring in through two open windows behind her. She was speaking to me from her apartment near Bondi Beach, she said, which explained her luminescent glow. She looked well. The kind of well that only people who live in close proximity to open water and who see the sun as a daily fact of life can.

'So,' she began, 'what made you want to start sex therapy?'

'There is something wrong with me,' I said. 'My friends, everyone I speak to, appears to find sex such an easy, fun part of life and I just don't. I think I'm broken.'

Growing up, everyone around me seemed to be having carefree, mind-blowing sex, I explained. When friends would tell me about the latest guy or girl they'd hooked up with, I would nod, wide-eyed and enthusiastic, wondering internally: *HOW? How can you not feel beset by worry every time you take off your clothes in front of someone? How can you not feel paralysed by anxiety when someone begins to slide your knickers down your thighs, terrified they're going to find you disgusting? That they are going to recoil in horror as they discover you have sharp teeth in place of a vagina, ready to clamp down on their unsuspecting penis the moment it enters you?*

OK, so I don't actually have teeth in my vulva, but I felt so embarrassed about how my body would be perceived by others, how it would taste and smell and look and feel, that I may as well have done. I felt ashamed of my body just as I felt ashamed of my inability to enjoy it the way others could.

At age 28, I was a stranger to my body. I tried to explain why. How my connection to sex was founded not on curiosity or exploration but, largely, on a perception of desire as something I needed to evoke in others rather than cultivate for myself. Informed by magazine articles telling me how to appeal to boys; TV shows depicting young girls obsessing over their male counterparts; romcoms that followed a woman in obsessive pursuit of her lover – I grew up seeking validation in male attention. I closely tied my sense of self-worth to being chosen by the boys I fancied and interpreted rejection in the face of my pursuits as confirmation of all the things I hated about myself. Since I believed that the boys picked the girls and then our job was to try to please them, I didn't consider myself a person with sexual agency. I had learned to prioritise the performance of pleasure for whoever decided to pick me as their one-time, sometime or long-time lover. I was just a girl, perennially standing in front of a boy, willing him to love her. Whatever happened next unfolded on his terms, not mine.

Perhaps my sex education, or lack thereof, was to blame. It consisted of two rules: 'Don't get pregnant and don't get an STI', followed by such a graphic video of a woman giving birth, it was enough to drive anyone to a life of pious chastity. I tried to fill the plentiful gaps left behind in my sexual knowledge through TV – my trusted source on everything outside of the classroom (I was a TV watcher of Olympic proportions), but whatever image of intimacy I garnered from such prestigious shows as *The O.C.*, *Gossip Girl* or *Boy*

*Meets World* was similarly lacking. They offered up the basic choreography of 'intimacy': the thrusting, the moaning, the way my body was supposed to move. But the sex I saw on screen was always depicted in a singular way – as a man penetrating a woman. And I was confused. Despite few, if any, words ever being exchanged, the two protagonists would always end up reaching some sort of sexual high in apparent unison, before collapsing into one another in shared post-coital (!) bliss. Why, then, did I fail to reach anything close to a euphoric sexual high every time a man stuck his dick in me? It had seldom occurred to me that my connection to my sexuality could 1) transcend men and 2) centre my own pleasure.

According to a 2007 study, there are 237 reasons why people have sex[8]. The researchers, from Texas University, who compiled the study noted at the start that this is an area of sexuality little investigated. Likely, they suggest, because scientists may, historically, have assumed that people have sex for a few simple reasons: to experience pleasure; to relieve tension; and to reproduce. Suspecting there was more to it, their study set out to create a broader and more comprehensive taxonomy of the motivations that drive people to have sex. The result is an extensive list of reasons showcasing just how complex and varied our general relationship to intimacy is. I recently flicked through the list and picked out the motivations that best described my own relationship to sex growing up. Amongst them: I was drunk; I wanted to have something to tell my friends; I was tired of being a virgin; I felt like it was my duty; I felt obligated to; I didn't know how to say 'no'; I didn't want to disappoint the person; it was expected of me.

I reflected on this selection of sex motivators, feeling a modicum of disappointment that it had never struck me to have sex in order to 'get closer to God', as it had to some participants in the study. I wondered whether those who had sex in this way were left disappointed in their reach for the Almighty. Or whether they had achieved a state of such ecstasy in orgasm it felt truly transcendent. *La petite mort*! Either way, the sex I described to Aleks during that first session felt nothing close to spiritual. Instead, it had been informed by a one-sided perception of male-centric intimacy that left little room for my own desires or feelings, whatever those were.

In 2023, the film *How to Have Sex* hit our screens, exploring the complexities of consent in British sex culture. The film was inspired by director Molly Manning-Walker's own experience navigating the formative years of her sex life. There had been little nuance in the conversations she and friends had shared about it growing up, so when 'bad stuff' happened, it went largely unacknowledged – they were all too busy bigging each other up. Problematic experiences were glossed over, since sex was considered through the lens of status – something to be celebrated rather than interrogated, no matter the context. Manning was herself sexually assaulted at age 16 when her drink was spiked on a night out. I spoke to her about it in an interview, just after the film was released, and she said if ever she brought it up in conversation, it felt immediately as though all the oxygen had been sucked out of the room. No one knows how to deal with sexual assault, she told me. Especially if you're young. Everyone just goes 'Fuck!' and then stops talking. She wrote the film as a way of challenging that silence and because she wanted to prompt a more in-depth conversation around consent.

And so, the film follows a trio of girls on their post-GCSE summer holiday to Malia, Crete, where, sun-kissed and experience-hungry, they ricochet between the pool, the bar, the club, briefly to bed, then back to the pool, the bar and the club again – rinse and repeat. You can feel the cheap liquor burn the back of your throat as you watch them chug away, chasing each night with the alacrity of a priest in search of the Holy Spirit. In true coming-of-age style, the least sexually experienced of the three, Tara (played by Mia McKenna-Bruce), is determined to have sex for the first time while they're away. Like me, her 'virginity' was a burden she wanted rid of – sex being the way she thinks she can discard the unwanted vestiges of her youth.

She ends up having sex with one of the boys they meet at the resort. Drunk on the beach, they kiss, then, as she tries to pull away, he presses himself on her more forcefully. She doesn't verbally say no, but her body is rigid and she's visibly uncomfortable. He pushes himself inside her regardless. When it's over, she quickly wipes away a tear so he doesn't see. The following day, her friends congratulate her on finally doing it, all while she struggles to process what happened, and to articulate why it felt so bad.

I watched the movie with my best friend, and we flinched in unison as we were confronted with scenes that felt all too familiar. I had been in Tara's position countless times before, uncomfortable with the way my body was being touched but unable to say anything. Lacking not only the words, but more importantly the confidence, to express to the person on top of me that it hurt; that it didn't feel as good as I knew it should; that I didn't want to do it. In a similar vein, Mia wants to have sex because she thinks it is what is expected of her – she wants what sex represents rather than sex itself. And that mismatch leaves her with no language at all for what she's actually feeling.

I turned to my friend. 'Does that guy remind you of Creepy Chris?' I asked her.

'Yes!' she responded immediately. 'It's strange to think back on how casually we dressed up sexual assault when we were young,' she thought aloud. It was always a big joke, wrapped up in disconcerting codenames for boys we all knew it was best to avoid. That guy would hug you from behind, then put his hands down your knickers without asking. His friend would pin you to the floor in a rugby tackle, amused by your screaming as his hands found their way to your crotch. Another would pull down your bra and tell everyone what he thought of your undeveloped boobs. 'Little grapes!' he'd say, laughing while your cheeks burned. 'Then do you remember that old guy who used to hang around the parties we went to? The one who had a thing for 15-year-olds? We all got with him because we thought he was cool – he was in a band – but what the hell was a 25-year-old doing getting with teenagers?'

The #MeToo movement, we agreed, had finally given us the language to make sense of sexual experiences that had harmed us. It had started a discussion we sorely needed on how sex, power and consent intersect, allowing us to understand for the first time that the shame we felt around things that had been done to us wasn't ours to bear. But it also exposed how desperately we needed something more: a sexual re-education that would help us not just to call out bad behaviour, but to more meaningfully start practicing consent. Because consent assumes a basic level of erotic literacy – the ability to read your body's signals, to know what you do and don't want, and to have the vocabulary and confidence to communicate that to someone else. Most of us were never taught that. I learned how to avoid pregnancy and STIs and could even put a condom on a banana. But, like Tara, I didn't know how I wanted to be touched. I didn't understand my sexuality well enough to know where my boundaries were. And, fundamentally, I didn't know how to say no because I'd never learned how to feel my yes – to understand desire outside of trying to be desired. When your idea of sexual participation looks more like acquiescence than agency, how meaningful is your ability to consent?

This lack of erotic literacy is a very specific kind of silencing – part of the long, patriarchal project that poet and classicist Anne Carson describes in *The Gender of Sound* (1994). She traces how, since antiquity, women's voices have been treated as unruly and in need of control. Sophocles, for example, described Echo – the talkative nymph punished by Hera until she could only repeat the words of others – as 'the girl with no door on her mouth', a figure whose voice had to be contained. As Carson writes, 'putting a door on the female mouth has been an important project of patriarchal culture from antiquity'. In a culture that has historically mistrusted women's voices, it makes sense that many of us grew up unable to articulate our desires, boundaries or discomfort. If consent is a kind of speech, erotic literacy requires the freedom to speak. But historically, women's voices have often been silenced.

'I guess I don't really know what I want from sex,' I told Aleks. 'Because I've never really thought about what sex actually means to me. I'm more concerned with doing it "wrong" than I am with enjoying it, so I always just focus on trying to make the other person feel good, without thinking about what I want, or how I feel. And now, I don't really feel anything. Sex has become a sort of perfunctory ode to intimacy, often without any sense of real connection. Without any real pleasure.'

My first sexual experience was at 12 years old, I told her. I was fingered at a party by a boy from the school next door. It hurt a lot, but I imagined it was my sexual inexperience as opposed to his rough touch that was to blame. Over the years that followed, I tried to get to know my body through the boys and men I gave it to. But in my desire to be desired, I had sex on other people's terms. I did it for what it symbolised rather than for how it felt, and now I felt at odds with my body.

Aleks looked at me sympathetically through the screen. 'It is totally normal,' she responded, 'to not want sex if the sex you're having is not sex you enjoy. I'm not surprised you feel disconnected from intimacy when so many of your earlier sexual experiences weren't great, and some much worse than that.

'Before we continue, could you tell me a little bit more about your relationship to your body?'

## Chapter 2

# Sex and the Beauty Myth

Two carrots

Three teaspoons hummus

One chunk of cheese

One bite chocolate

For over a decade, I kept a daily list of everything I'd eaten that day. Often I'd rewrite the list over and over again, transferring it to Post-it notes which I would stick around my room or absentmindedly leave out in the kitchen, only to realise ashamedly sometime later that my mum had tidied these little scraps of incriminating paper away. Like so many young women today, I grew up with an eating disorder, which started around the age of 12. I went to an all-girls' school where starving yourself was cool and getting diagnosed with anorexia was a badge of honour, so it was perhaps of little surprise that I eventually toed the party line and shrunk my tall frame into a shrivelled shell of a girl's body.

It started like so many adolescent eating disorders do, with friends and I deciding together to embark on a variety of diets we'd read about in magazines. We'd eat just fruit for several days at a time, then relish entire loaves of bread when finally our days of grapes and slivers of kiwi were over. We'd obsessively sprinkle chilli powder over everything on our plates because an article suggested chilli helps to burn additional calories, all while purchasing every and any diet product going, forever taken in by the promise of LOW-FAT this and LOW-SUGAR that. As new fads came in and out of fashion, we'd continually write and then rewrite our list of prohibited food groups, moving from no-carb to fat-free to sans sugar with the burning hope that if only we could get the next diet right, we'd finally have bodies we'd like, bodies we could bear.

It was 2004, and the size-zero trend was taking over Hollywood. Every female celebrity either looked like a lollipop – bug-eyed and bobble-headed, their hungry eyes crying out 'feed me!' from behind giant, saucer-like glasses – or else was branded 'fat' by the tabloids. Magazine covers would regularly show mean red circles highlighting areas of 'celeb cellulite' that had been cruelly zoomed in on and magnified for our perverse pleasure. And the catwalks and fashion shoots we'd ogle in *Vogue* or *Elle* featured exclusively pin-thin, white models, many of whom I had plastered across my schoolroom locker next to notes reminding myself: DO

NOT EAT. I wanted to be a lollipop lady like the women in the magazines, like the women in the sad YouTube videos I started watching every night before bed, which showed depressing montages of the Olsen twins and Nicole Richie looking hollow-eyed and rail-thin, set to a backing track of Imogen Heap's 'Hide and Seek'.

I longed to look as they did and felt repulsed by the roll of fat that sat stubbornly around my own midriff. From age eight I started writing letters to Father Christmas asking for combat trousers, belly tops and a thin tummy I could proudly bare. And every morning of the 25th when I woke up looking exactly the same as the night before, my heart sank, disappointment flooding through my bones. All I wanted was to be thin because being thin was good. Being thin meant being desirable, disciplined, attractive, palatable. It would show the world that I had self-restraint. That my body wasn't as unruly as my mind and that I too was destined for success. Because successful people were thin. Pretty people were thin. The deities we worshipped in their Hollywood mansions, they were all so goddamn thin.

Often, while falling asleep at night, I'd imagine someone offering me dollops of chocolate from a giant tablespoon and promising me that with every single bite I'd lose a few more pounds. How intensely dull a pre-teen fantasy to have buried in my adolescent mind. But I'm a millennial woman who grew up in the cult of thinness. I cannot remember a time when I didn't worry about my body, when I didn't cast mean, criticising eyes over a body that was just trying to get me through the day.

In *Girl On Girl: How Pop Culture Turned a Generation of Women Against Themselves* (2025), journalist Sophie Gilbert reminds us afresh of how pernicious the messaging buried within the cultural iconography of the early 2000s was, particularly when it came to women's bodies. This was the era, Gilbert explains, in which we saw the explosion of a genre of television that weaponised the insecurity of young girls in order to sell us things: things we didn't know existed, to address problems we didn't know we had, all in the name of the newly sanctified version of perfection.

This was, after all, the period of 'The Transformation', she argues. Evidenced by the explosion of makeover shows like *The Swan* (2004), in which women beset by anguish at their own appearance were subject to drastic makeovers involving numerous cosmetic procedures, the results of which were only revealed to the contestants during the show's finale; until then, mirrors were banned. And *America's Next Top Model* (2003–2018), in which women were chided for not having sufficient thigh gaps and encouraged to go on extreme diets if they wanted a real shot at modelling fame. Such shows went hand in hand with the growing popularity of diet books like *Diet Revolution* and *French Women Don't Get Fat* (2004), to convince a generation of women that they, that we, were forever just a few pounds and tweakments away from a better version of ourselves. It was tantalising, this idea that perfection could not just be achieved, but bought. That, with the right products, the right diet, the right procedures, we could all go through the sort of life overhaul that turned Anne Hathaway in *The Princess Diaries* (2001) from ugly duckling to boy-magnet royalty. And, of course, as her hair was rendered less frizzy, her glasses removed, the rest of her life was transformed too. The message was clear. When you improve how you look, everything else is elevated with it.

Leading the charge on the pull of The Transformation were, of course, the celebrities living in their fishbowls, increasingly visible to the rest of us through the eyes of the internet and the spectator sport of reality TV. I remember vividly watching with thrilled horror as *The Hills'* girl next door Heidi Montag transformed herself into a real-life Barbie during season six of the show, undergoing as many as ten cosmetic surgeries in a single day. She was just 23.

There was a perverse fascination in witnessing such a drastic makeover in what felt like real time. Heidi was the personification of the compulsion to pursue perfection at *all costs*. It was an endeavour not only encouraged, but validated, by a popular culture increasingly obsessed with the before and after, with the fat now thin, ugly now hot, lame now cool. The results may have been shocking, but I couldn't look away. Suddenly, everything I hated about myself felt additionally incriminating and eminently fixable. The full-body transformation was an irresistible notion to a young teenager already at war with themselves and fluent in the language of self-hate.

That I, and so many women around me, grew up fixated

on the size of our bodies and the contours of our faces is, according to author Naomi Wolf, no accident. In her seminal book, *The Beauty Myth*, published in 1990, Wolf argues that throughout history, a reductive ideal of female beauty has been deeply entrenched within Western society, urging women to believe that to be considered attractive (read: socially acceptable) we must change how we look, alter our size, perfect our complexion. Since the industrial revolution, she writes, the ideology of beauty has become an increasingly potent political force, assuming the work of social coercion that myths around motherhood, domesticity, chastity, and passivity could no longer sustain. While second-wave feminism had gone some way towards diminishing the hold these myths exerted over women's lives, liberating us from the idea that our time should be spent exclusively in the kitchen, our destiny typified by child-rearing, an alternative ideology took over. One centred on notions of beauty. 'It is a dark vein of self-hatred, physical obsessions, terror of aging, and dread of lost control,' she writes.

Looking back, Montag was in many ways a bellwether for the normalisation of an increasingly extreme regime of beauty. One propelled forward by a new and more advanced system for the dissemination of ideology: social media. Filters made possible the instant (digital) transformation of anyone with a phone, populating the digital world with our perfected pixelated doubles. Meanwhile, the growing accessibility of plastic surgery made 'Instagram face' attainable on a far wider scale. The result is an aesthetic homogeneity measured on a scale of Kardashian-likeness. The increasingly monolithic presentation of female beauty serves as a very literal representation of the Beauty Myth's organising principle. How many women have been persuaded to alter their faces in line with standards engineered by a beauty industrial complex designed for one purpose: profit. And who controls that industry? Mostly men. A 2022 report found that more than 65% of executive committee seats in beauty companies are held by men.[9]

After years of chasing punishing beauty regimes, and knowing all too well that pleasure is seldom found in the perfection of my reflection, the ubiquity of this new standard of augmented beauty remains hard to resist. I still feel sucked in by the allure of the cyborgian ideal. Convinced, on less confident days, that life really could be a bit better if only I had a smaller nose, a more sculpted face, a tauter jawline. No amount of feminist literature is sufficient to insulate me entirely from the ideology of beauty. Particularly as it becomes wrapped up in the discourse of self-care and wellness. The body is a project upon which we must constantly be working. In cryochambers, on juice cleanses, with Botox and even salmon sperm. In today's visual culture, the image has been elevated to one of the highest forms of cultural capital. But as we've reified our pixelated form, we've denigrated our actual bodies.

I recoil at the thought of how much of my life I have spent worrying about the way I look, about the size of my thighs, the shape of my tummy, those laughter lines I feel I ought to freeze out of existence. How much of our collective headspace has been taken up obsessing over these perceived imperfections when instead we might be thinking about something, *anything*, else? Regressive policymaking and heavy-handed laws are one way to clamp down on women's freedom, but another, far more insidious and pernicious way is to get into our heads and infect our minds with the ideology of perfectionism. As Wolf put it: 'a culture fixated on female thinness is not an obsession about female beauty' at all; it is one obsessed with female *obedience*. 'Dieting is the most potent political sedative in women's history,' she writes, because 'a quietly mad population is a tractable one.'

In her essay 'Foucault, Femininity, and the Modernization of Patriarchal Power',[10] philosopher Sandra Lee Bartky raises this very point as she argues that women's bodies have been shaped by the 'obsessions and preoccupations' of their cultural moment, notably through narrow, rigid ideals of femininity. The 'tyranny of slenderness', she writes, is its own modern disciplinary regime, pitting women against their own needs in a purposefully fraught pursuit: the ideal we're told to chase is always an unattainable one. You're never going to be thin enough, beautiful enough, good enough – not least because the beauty standard is forever changing, and with it, the direction in which our mental energy and body punishment is directed.

Consider the rise in Brazilian butt lifts (BBLs): between 2015 and 2019, procedures increased by over 90%,[11] making it one of the fastest-growing cosmetic surgeries in the world.

All while remaining the most dangerous, with early studies suggesting a mortality rate as high as 1 in 3,000.[12] And for what? To chase an aesthetic shaped by Kardashian curves and algorithmic approval – an ideal that, like all the others before it, is already beginning to fall out of favour. What happens, then, to the plastic-bottomed women who risked their lives to build their bodies in the image of a trend, when the ideal begins again to change?

But this is the point. Femininity, as Bartky says, fundamentally operates as a spectacle we're required to perform. Every time a woman smooths her hair, sucks in her stomach, scans her reflection for flaws, injects herself with Ozempic or heads to the clinic for a plastic butt . . . she's doing the work of the self-policing subject. She is monitoring her body and appearance for a world that has convinced her she is fundamentally flawed. Diet culture is just the system through which women are trained to watch themselves, to shrink themselves, to punish themselves for falling short of a perfection that doesn't exist. And every time we inevitably fail and fall short of the impossible ideal, the shame pushes us to try harder – to be more disciplined, more self-denying, more in control.

This brings to mind a conversation I recently had with an old colleague.

We were at a mutual friend's birthday party and catching up on some 10 years' worth of life news. We'd never been close, but I'd observed her from a distance to be someone who seemed self-assured. She had been quiet, almost aloof, lending the impression of someone several years older than she really was. One of the smartest women in the newsroom at the time, she'd also been one of the most beautiful. But as we spoke now, she told me that, despite being pregnant, she was still measuring her body daily – her waist and hips and thighs – and lambasting herself for the increased inches, despite knowing this to be a necessary part of growing a baby.

'Measuring yourself?' I asked, unsure whether this was perhaps a pregnancy thing I was unaware of.

'Yes,' she responded bluntly. She had measured her body with a tape measure every single day for as long as she could remember, hating herself every time she saw even the most marginal increase in the numbers. It's a form of self-abuse, she admitted, but she couldn't stop.

Now eight months pregnant, these numbers had increased significantly, as was to be expected, but it had destroyed her confidence and fostered a whole new level of self-consciousness about her body. She could no longer bear her partner touching her, despite how often he reassured her that she was beautiful, that her pregnant body was glowing, that she should stop worrying about gaining a bit of weight while growing another human. She couldn't hear it. And so they'd stopped having sex, she admitted. She missed the intimacy, but she couldn't stand feeling present in her pregnant body; it was just too unbearable.

Our societal obsession with women's thinness is about obedience, yes, but it is obedience cultivated through separating women from themselves. From pitting us against our bodies, so that we focus the anger and frustration we inevitably feel at perceiving ourselves as inadequate on to our own seemingly untameable bodies, rather than directing it at the system that convinced us we were broken in the first place.

And so the Beauty Myth doesn't just affect our self-confidence, causing us to turn in and on ourselves instead of out into the world. It affects the way we relate to, and hence experience, our own bodies.

The Beauty Myth disrupts our connection to pleasure.

## In pursuit of perfection, I built myself a cage

'Well, you aren't a very happy bunny, are you?' the male doctor said to me as he ticked some more boxes on the form in front of him. 'I am diagnosing you with mild depression and anorexia nervosa. You'll be referred to a separate clinic for treatment.' I had just turned 13 years old.

That morning, before leaving for the appointment, I'd written a note in my diary that read something like: 'Today I am going to get diagnosed with an eating disorder, then this can all be over.' I remember putting pen to paper with crystal clarity. Resolved in my determination to win what had been designated among my peers as this ultimate badge of honour. The rot that is this disease is ugly. It's grotesque. It propels you to do things to your body you wouldn't wish on anyone. To become so self-obsessed as to forget there is a world outside of your own pocket of personal pain.

I looked at the doctor, his glasses balanced precariously at the end of his nose as he stared at me with an expression of what? Pity? Or was it disgust? How many young girls walked through his door each week, taking up his time with their self-inflicted disorders that led to self-inflicted wounds that meant he had to be the bearer of bad news to concerned parents waiting just outside the door. Well, yes, she is sick. No, it is not a sickness of the body so much as a sickness of the mind that is in turn destroying her body. And yes, unfortunately, anorexia has the highest mortality rate of any psychiatric disorder, so there is a chance your daughter will die. Sorry, sorry. An inconvenient truth. But on the bright side, all she needs to do is JUST EAT.

I looked down.

*Huh*, I thought to myself. *Well, I guess I've made it.* I've reached the finish line in the race I'm competing in against myself. In the full-body 'Transformation' I'd been lured into pursuing at, well, all costs. Was this success? It didn't feel like a victory but more like a trap. And now I was here, I didn't know how to stop running. I didn't know how to get back to the person I'd wanted to run from.

I thought about the friends who'd tried to help, who brought salad pots to my desk every lunch while I sat there alone pretending I could read through the brain fog and telling anyone who asked, 'I'm not hungry. Huge breakfast . . .'

I thought about my mum, who'd brought me porridge every morning while I got ready for school, knowing full well that it would be untouched when I left.

I thought too of my dad, typically stoic in the face of

adversity, his shell hardened from having lost his own dad at just 12, who'd broken down and wept just days earlier. Unable to look at me without feeling he was about to lose another person he loved so very deeply and whose life he had just wanted to protect.

But the problem with an eating disorder is that once it's taken root in your brain, you lose a little bit of yourself – the bit that lends perspective on what is pain you can endure and what is pain that might kill you; the bit that reminds you of who you are outside of this thing that's somehow become your whole identity; the bit that cautions you not to go too close to the edge because, really, it's not worth it. In its place is a voice that says you're *still* not enough. That tells you all you have left is this body you no longer recognise and over which you cannot, must not, relinquish control. You feel trapped in the mental cage you've built for yourself.

Because that is exactly what this is: a mental cage you construct for yourself with the tools handed to you by a society bent on shrinking women so small they don't disrupt the order. It's not really self-inflicted, is it? A starving woman is a subservient woman, after all. Or at least one so distractedly introspective as to pose no threat to a regime of thought that says her position ought never to be one of power.

So you continue building. At first, you designate certain foods as bad and off-limits. A few pillars are erected. Then you start to develop routines and regimes that allow you to avoid situations in which you might be tempted, or expected, to eat. A few more pillars go up. Then you devise increasingly weird eating habits to avoid actually eating: you pick at food and push it around your plate; you drink milk and crunch on ice cubes to quell your hunger; you hide food underneath other bits of food so you can pretend to yourself that everyone thinks you're eating. Several more pillars go up. You spend increasing amounts of time alone because you're tired and, besides, no one really wants to hang out with you now anyway. Another pillar.

And then one day you look up at the clock and it's only 1pm and you're so exhausted you wonder how you're going to make it to the end of the (school) day. You wonder whether you'll make it to tomorrow because there's no energy left in the reserves. There's nothing left. It's at that moment you realise you're living in the cage you built for yourself. You've shrunk your world so that all you can see is those goddamn pillars, and while they were meant to give you control, you've never felt so out of control in your life. You're on a treadmill that's going faster and faster, but there are no buttons to make it all just STOP. So what else is there to do then but just keep on running?

## A reputation to maintain

Several months later, I was called into the headmistress's office at school. While I may have felt trapped in my cage, I was still visible to the world around me, apparently. And my visibility, or what my body represented, was now a problem. It was the other parents, you see. Unbeknown to them, we – me and their girls – had been in this together. We had drunk from the cultural tap in unison, imbibing the poison that infected our minds and made us believe there was only one way to be a Good Woman: thin. We had run to the toilet as one to purge the contents of our stomachs in protest against our disobedient bodies' urge for nourishment. We had dieted together. We had fawned over anorexic stars together. We had done this all *together*. But now I was the problem. A bad influence. A rotten apple. The source of the poison from which their children drank. Something had to be done.

'You have several weeks to start eating again – something, anything! – or else we will have to suspend you. It won't go on your record – you haven't done anything *wrong* per se – but I'd have to ask that you don't return until you're better.'

It didn't look good having anorexic girls walking in and out of a school renowned for fostering a culture of eating disorders, did it? What would people say? What would people think?

That evening, on my bus journey home, I leaned my head against the window and cried as I watched south-east London speeding by beneath me, the rest of the world oblivious to the inner turmoil raging within another starving girl's body. Is this it? I wondered. Is this the promised land? The reward for achieving the body, the discipline, the supposed self-restraint that I'd idealised in the size-zero pin-ups strewn across my magazines, across the tabloids, across the gossip sites I lapped up hungrily at break? I suppose that's the trap of the myth of perfection as we've connected it to being thin. It compels us to sacrifice our mind, our health and our spirit at the altar of the ideal body, but in return there is nothing close to heavenly reward.

It dawned on me then, as I sat on the bus, just how much I'd lost. No friends, poor grades, thin hair, no period. And my body – God, it hurt. From the moment I woke up until the moment I went to bed, I was cold. I felt cold in my bones. I felt cold right at the core of my body, where it seemed as though the furnace had been switched off and all evidence of life had been extinguished. If I was forced to leave school, I would be left with nothing resembling a normal life. I would have no way of distracting myself from this feeling of emptiness. The thought was overwhelming.

And so that day something inside of me switched; one of the pillars fell down and through the crack a beam of light came in. Over the coming weeks and months I gradually began to eat. I stopped weighing myself daily and started to sit down for mealtimes with friends and family. At first, it felt humiliating, as though I was admitting to everyone around me that I had been defeated, that I'd somehow failed. But over time I began to appreciate just how much I'd missed the way mealtimes punctuate each part of the day.

When in the throes of illness, I'd lost track of time as I'd lost track of my place in it, wafting between a detached engagement with my surroundings and the mental thicket in which I'd become ensnared. As I started to eat, and even enjoy, food again, I felt as though I'd crossed back over to the realm of the living. No longer suspended in my limbo of self-destruction, I remembered what it felt like to have the energy to think beyond the minute in front of me. To feel warmth in my body, and fire in my veins. But an eating disorder is a mental illness more than it is a physical one, and mental illnesses are not so easily cured. I had a rot in my brain that continued to fester.

## Overeaters Anonymous

When I was in my early twenties, long before I started sex therapy, I went to a single Overeaters Anonymous meeting. It took place in the basement of a beautiful church somewhere in Marylebone, a detail I remember because I lingered outside for some 20 or so minutes, pacing up and down the pavement before eventually forcing myself to walk through the doors. I'd found the meeting on the recommendation of a friend, who had similarly harboured an eating disorder since her teenage years. Whenever she was stressed, she'd rely on being sick to temporarily relieve her anxiety, only to become locked in another vicious cycle of bingeing and purging — a habit as anxiety-inducing as it was temporarily soothing. I knew that merry-go-round well. But these sessions helped, she told me — at the very least they provided her with the comfort of knowing she wasn't alone in what felt like self-imposed mania. I agreed to give one a try.

I was in a particularly violent rut of making myself sick at the time. Just a few weeks prior, I'd given myself a black eye through the force with which I'd made myself retch, rupturing a stye in the corner of my eyelid. I told friends the stye had burst of its own accord, and no one noticed the line of small bruises that simultaneously covered my knuckles. I took perverse satisfaction in observing these self-inflicted battle wounds. They made me feel connected to my body in an odd sort of way. Like a shared secret connecting two strangers.

I walked downstairs to join my fellow self-abusers in search of relief and found an empty chair at the back of the room. I felt self-conscious. The meeting began, and members of the OE congregation took it in turns to introduce themselves and their specific assortment of eating disorders, before launching into whatever related issue they'd been struggling with of late. Just as those attending an AA meeting are encouraged to refer to themselves as alcoholics, regardless of how long they've been sober, we were advised to do the same. To speak of our illness in the present. 'Hi, I'm Emma-Louise and I'm an anorexic and a bulimic,' I announced to the room.

There are many parallels[13] between substance addiction and anorexia: compulsive behaviour patterns despite the obvious harm they cause; a narrowing of one's behavioural repertoire around the disordered behaviour/habit; a preoccupation and ritualisation around food, body and weight akin to the addict's substance seeking/use. Anorexia and addiction also share similar reward and control pathways in the brain, driving the same cycles of obsession, anxiety relief and compulsive behaviour. There are also many differences. For one, the anorexic is not addicted to any chemical substance, so there is no external dependence to break free from. This makes recovery a very different proposition for the addict versus the anorexic, since the former must often go cold turkey in order to beat the addiction, while the latter cannot just give up food. The anorexic has to re-establish their relationship to the very things they perceive themselves to be at war with: food and their body. All while living in daily communion/confrontation with both.

It makes sense, then, to self-describe as *an anorexic* as a way of acknowledging that recovery is always a work in progress – the illness remains within you and you are forever trying to navigate what 'normalcy' is supposed to look and feel like. But I resented these labels. I didn't identify with either moniker. Sure, I had a troubled relationship with food and my body, but these terms felt constricting. Or perhaps I just wasn't ready to bear the weight of what they conferred.

A few years ago I came across a study[14] that suggested even after physical recovery, the brains of people who've experienced anorexia may continue to process pleasure and reward differently. Many of us become exceptionally good at self-denial – at overriding appetite, discomfort and even pleasure – all in service of the larger project at hand: getting thinner. That same capacity can later reappear as other forms of self-punishing discipline: relentless exercise, workaholism, the compulsive need to achieve. One must try to fill the void somehow.

In the study, researchers used fMRI scans to see how participants responded to winning or losing small amounts of money – a basic reward-and-loss task. Women who had been 'recovered' for at least a year (normal weight, regular periods, no active symptoms) showed something striking: their brains responded almost the same way to both winning and losing. In healthy controls, the reward circuits lit up clearly for wins. In the recovered group, that difference was blunted.

What this suggests is that anorexia doesn't just change the body; it can leave a long-lasting imprint on how the brain processes reward. A 'recovered' brain may lean more heavily on control (planning, monitoring, managing) than spontaneous pleasure. It's not that we can't feel good, only that pleasure may become something we have to consciously practise rather than something that arrives automatically. Something we have to actively reclaim.

I thought about this research when I interviewed somatic sexologist Aisha Paris Smith. Like me, Aisha grew up with an eating disorder that started in her teenage years. She suffered emotional trauma in her childhood, she explained, when she was exposed to domestic violence, and took on the role of rescuer amid the instability of her home environment. At 16 she left home, and it was then that she developed an eating disorder – what she described as her body finally beginning to show the stress and trauma it had absorbed over the preceding years. It's like when you've been working incessantly, she explained, and then you finally go on holiday and immediately get sick. 'It's because at last your body has space to share and communicate how it's been impacted, and how your resources have been depleted.

'I was "happiest," she reflected, 'when my body was completely submissive, which was always the result of the exhaustion of either starving myself or purging.'

This went on for years until, sometime in her early twenties, she quit her job and went travelling around Asia. She met a man who introduced her to a sex-positive community and it was then that something began, finally, to shift. Surrounded by people who were practicing tantric yoga and exploring conscious sexuality, she started experimenting with tantric sex herself and feeling present in her body for the first time. This required a fundamental recalibration regarding how she connected to pleasure, she said – something she'd learned to mistrust because it all too often led to binges, 'because it had become hedonistic'. In learning to enjoy sex, she was able to repair her relationship to pleasure and her body. It was the impact of this experience that prompted her, years later, to train to become a sexological bodyworker – a somatic practitioner who helps people explore sexual pleasure and embodiment. Now, her lived experience gives her a greater depth of understanding and ability to support others.

After our conversation, I thought about what Aisha had said about distrusting pleasure when she feared it would tip into excess. And I thought about all the women I knew who were in a battle with their bodies – women who were always monitoring, restricting and admonishing themselves for their size. It occurred to me then that while my brain had been primed to prioritise discipline over delight, diet culture continued to reinforce the very instincts I was trying to unlearn. It taught me, as it taught the women around me, that our worth lies in our ability to shrink ourselves. If the demonisation of women's voices is one way of robbing us of power, then severing us from our bodies is another. The door on our mouths is a door on our bodies, too. I never went back to another Overeaters Anonymous because I couldn't bear to announce myself to the room through a label I refused to connect with. Five or more years later, sitting across from Aleks, I recognised I still had a problem. Only by acknowledging it could I move forward.

Hi, I'm Emma-Louise and I'm an anorexic and a bulimic.


## You can't enjoy sexual pleasure in a body that you hate

'For as long as you're at war with your body, Emma, you're going to struggle to enjoy sex. Think about it. If your experience of pleasure happens in your body,' Aleks said in our next therapy session, 'but you're in a body that you hate, then how are you supposed to access pleasure? How do you expect a body that you're punishing continually to provide you with orgasms?'

I looked down at my thighs, thinking about all the many years I'd spent despising them and wondered, not for the first time, what it might feel like not to spend one's life fixated on your thigh gap.

'People come to sex therapy thinking it's going to be light and fluffy and sexy, and I'm just going to tell you to do X-Y-Z and then suddenly you'll be able to have sex like a porn star,' Aleks continued. 'But it's not that at all. If you hold the belief that no person will ever think you're good enough during sex if you have tummy rolls, for example, then you can have all the orgasm tips in the world but you're still going to have a hard time connecting to your body.'

I had never before considered how my relationship to my body had affected my connection to sex. Perhaps because I didn't think of sex as something embodied. It was something done to my body rather than something I experienced in connection to it. So, it had never really occurred to me that my inability to orgasm might be related to the punishing lens through which I saw myself. Now, it seemed so obvious.

Aleks Trkulja didn't set out to become a sex therapist. She was studying psychology as an undergraduate student at the University of Sydney and finding the contents of her course somewhat dry when one day in 2014 she stumbled across sex therapy as an intriguing area within the field of mental health. It immediately piqued her interest, and she applied for an internship with sex therapist Tanya Koens, who was working locally in Sydney. When Aleks arrived at their office for her first day on the job, Tanya suggested they begin with a breathing exercise and pulled up a video on their phone depicting an anus expanding and contracting. 'Match your breath to the pace of the anus,' Tanya instructed.

As they sat there inhaling and exhaling to the rhythm of this virtual anus, Tanya turned to Aleks and noted, 'If you can breathe to an anus, that's great, because it is just another body part and not something we should feel any shame about.' It was Aleks's first lesson in tackling sexual shame. And she was hooked. A few years later, she wrote her Master's thesis on counselling and mental health, looking specifically at sexual dysfunction and how it is interconnected with body image. There hasn't been nearly enough research into this over the years, she later tells me – there never is when it comes to issues notably pertaining to women's bodies – but there is growing evidence to support what now feels glaringly obvious: that how we connect to our bodies impacts on the way we connect to and experience sex. She pointed me in the direction of the couple we have in large part to thank for this.

In the 1950s and 1960s, sex researchers Virginia Johnson and William Masters changed the way human sexuality was understood in America, and indeed the rest of the world. Their work followed on the heels of biologist Dr Alfred Kinsey (after whom the present-day Kinsey Institute is named), who, during the two decades prior, had explored the varieties of human sexual experience by way of thousands of interviews documenting people's sexual histories. Kinsey's research was groundbreaking, challenging conventional wisdom around 'normal sexual behaviour' (nearly all the so-called sexual perversions fall within the range of biological normality, he argued[15]), while providing a litany of revelations about the prevalence of masturbation, adultery and premarital sex, orgasms and homosexuality.

But Masters and Jonhson were more scientific in their approach. They pioneered research into the *physiology* of human sexuality, i.e. what's actually happening in our bodies when we become sexually aroused. In practice, that meant they had the rather unique job of observing hundreds of men and women as they had sex or masturbated, monitoring how each person's body responded through various bits of psycho-physiological machinery. Masters was keen, apparently,[16] to interrogate certain attitudes surrounding the sexual experience that were prolific at the time, including the 1758 claim made by Swiss researcher Simon Andre that masturbation caused blindness, or else the suggestion that orgasm was more debilitating and potentially destructive to the body than a day spent in the fields, as per Elizabeth Osgood Willard's research in the 19th century.

Imagine the world's surprise when their research came up with different insights entirely.

Chief among their own findings was the idea that anxiety is the root cause of most sexual dysfunctions. This was a bit of a revelation at the time, because it ran contrary to Freud's pathologisation of sexual issues, which he largely attributed to unconscious conflicts, repression or early childhood experiences. Everything, as it concerned women, seemed to lead back to 'hysteria' or unresolved psychosexual development in Freud's eyes. And as charming as that all was, Masters and Johnson's research gave us a new lens through which to see sexual difficulties, one which removed the stigma surrounding difficulty orgasming, and said that rather than this being a fixed psychological disorder (you're broken!), it was instead something that could be treated with behavioural therapy (you're not broken!).

Contributing to the anxiety people sometimes feel during sex was, they found, a phenomenon known as 'spectatoring' – a term they coined to describe the process whereby a person watches him or herself 'from a third-person perspective' during sex. Rather than focusing on the delicious sensations and feelings that come with being entangled in another's body, said spectator instead zooms out on the experience to judge how they look and how they're 'performing'. It's a subtle form of dissociation, where attention is directed towards self-monitoring rather than sensation. Numerous studies have since linked negative body image and this notion of spectatoring with sexual function, highlighting how significant a role self-image plays in our sexual desire, arousal and ability simply to stay present long enough to enjoy the sex we're having. In one such study, author Professor Virginia Ramseyer Winter concludes that 'negatively perceived body image is correlated to sexual malfunction for people engaging in hookups, but also that positively perceived body image is correlated to increased pleasure during sexual activities.' In other words, if you hate your body, you're more likely to feel self-conscious during intimacy, distracted by negative thoughts about what your body looks like. Whereas if you like your body, you're more likely to enjoy sex. Go figure.

Reading this, a thought occurred to me. Official statistics suggest that 700,000 women in the UK have an eating disorder,[17] and this is probably a pretty conservative figure given that number only reflects those who have sought professional help. (I don't know about you, but I know very few women who don't have some sort of complex relationship with their bodies.) So, I wondered, how many women are having disconnected, unpleasurable sex because they hate their bodies? Or because they have grown so used to viewing their bodies from an external, critical perspective, they don't know how to just *enjoy* their bodies? They don't know how to just *be* in their bodies?

In the course of my research, I googled something along the lines of 'how many women don't enjoy sex' and was met with a litany of articles discussing the 'orgasm gap': the disparity between the rate at which men versus women orgasm in heteronormative partnered sex. While studies show that men reliably orgasm some 95% of the time whether masturbating or having sex with a partner, their female counterparts reach climax just 65% of the time in the context of a relationship[18] – a figure that drops to just 18% during casual hookups, according to sex therapist Dr Karen Gurney.[19] Gurney would later tell me during an interview that the notable lack of an orgasm gap within same-sex couples shows that this is not an anatomical issue, as is sometimes suggested ('it's just harder to make a woman come!'), but rather a cultural issue regarding whose pleasure we've learned to prioritise. And, I added, who has been *conditioned* to live at war with their bodies and thus at odds with their pleasure.

I realised then that armies of women, like me, were struggling with their connection to sex. Far from being alone in this problem, I was actually in very good company. I felt relieved. But that relief was short-lived, sullied as it was by a subsequent realisation: the issues I was experiencing during sex were systemic rather than personal. A reflection of our wider, broken sex culture as opposed to my own private war. My frustrations began to curdle into the nascent buds of rage.

I quickly grabbed a pen and paper and started to write a list of bullet points in my notebook. All the things I thought were true about sex and my body but which I was now beginning to question.

Sex Myths I No Longer Believe . . .

- My body doesn't work as it's meant to
- Sex is for a man's pleasure rather than my own
- Sex is a performance
- It is harder to make a woman come, hence women don't often come during sex

'This is the only body you get,' Aleks reminded me as we wrapped up the session. 'This is your home for life. You don't get to trade it in for an upgrade, or decide, "Actually, I want a different model." So you have to decide whether you're going to punish your body forever, or whether you're going to forgive it, whether you're going to move on and allow it to be free to access pleasure. You cannot have both.

'And so the real work, if you want to start mending your relationship to sex, is to begin with your body.'

My mind wandered to an interview I'd read with writer and journalist Caitlin Moran years ago, in which she admitted she'd struggled to make any sort of peace with her body until around 34 years old. Like so many women around her, she'd grown up hating her body: every roll, every squishy part, every segment of her physical being that felt so out of step with the ideal to which she'd been programmed to aspire. But something shifted as she approached her mid-thirties, when, lying in bed one day, she looked down at her body and, instead of feeling the usual burning sense of animosity, she felt something different. She felt admiration, patting her legs and her tummy as she congratulated these various body parts for having birthed two children, for having carried her through each day.

Could I experience such a shift without needing to endure a 48-hour labour followed by an emergency C-section?

Sitting across from Aleks in our virtual therapy room, I was once again being presented with two options. I could continue as I was, treating my body as though it was enemy number one – cooking and eating only to throw up; exercising until I was in pain and taking laxatives until I was empty. But by staying at war with my body, I'd continue to struggle to orgasm and remain at odds with my body's capacity for sexual enjoyment. Or I could put down my weaponry, raise my white flag and attempt to make some semblance of peace with my body, if for no other reason than to exchange pain for the possibility of pleasure.

That day, something began to shift.

## Chapter 3

# The dictates of performed desirability

The first time a man asked me what I liked in bed, I was 25 years old. It was a casual hookup with a boy in a band – someone I knew fairly well and had fancied from the moment we met. As we lay together in the dark trying to make sense of one another's unfamiliar bodies, he whispered into my ear: 'Tell me what you like and what you want me to do to you.' I was dumbstruck. I had no idea. No one had ever asked me that question before and, more importantly, I had never asked it of myself either. Sex was something I just sort of did and didn't much think or talk about. It was also something I considered entirely relational, by which I mean I had no sexual relationship with my body outside of the context of sleeping with someone. I had invested little to no time exploring my vulva and felt uncomfortable at the mere thought of touching my own clitoris.

Unsure how to respond, I threw the question back to my one-night-stand-boy-in-a-band in the only way I knew how: 'No, what do youuuuuuu like,' I purred, imagining myself a sultry sex goddess about to give yet another performance of a lifetime.

And it worked. We spent the rest of the evening following his sexual script – probably as broken and riddled with shame in its own way as mine – while his question niggled in the back of my mind.

*What did I want?*

It was a question, I realised, several years later, I still couldn't answer. Something I heard writer Glennon Doyle say on her podcast surfaced in my mind: 'We [women] get so many confusing messages about our bodies, we don't see our bodies. We've been so used to being objectified, we objectify ourselves.' The result? 'We only know how to be desired. We don't know how to desire. We only know how to be wanted; we don't know how to want.'

The lesson in performed desirability is one instilled in young girls early on. Like a silent agreement struck the moment we are deemed attractive to a man and summoned for the pleasure of his gaze. I recall the first time I felt aware of such a contract. I was 11 years old and standing in front of an ice-cream van trying to decide what to pick.

'If we get a 99 Flake, will you give us an extra stick of chocolate for free?' my friend said, laughing and batting her eyelids in the way of a self-conscious pre-teen attempting the amateur art of seduction.

'If you both show me your boobs, *including your nipples*, I'll give you an ice cream for free,' he responded bluntly.

We giggled and blushed, suddenly aware of the triangle of trainer bra perched across each of our flat chests. 'Fuck off,' my friend retorted, grabbing my hand as she dragged me away to shouts of 'Come on! Just a quick flash!'

We laughed our way to a nearby corner store to buy a Cornetto instead, but the seed of an idea had been planted in my head: *Your body is something men want. Your body is something men will give you things in order to gain access to.* The thought made me feel uneasy.

At 15, I worked out that this silent contract could be financially lucrative. I had started waitressing, at weddings mainly, sometimes at funerals, and it was there that I learned how to wear my desirability in a way that guaranteed a crisp £20 note would be popped down my uniform-black shirt by the end of an evening – usually courtesy of an old man with wine-stained lips. He'd have spent the night conjuring a pseudo-intimacy between us: 'amiably' making me the butt of his jokes every time I approached the table, patting my bum as I walked off to refill their wine and commenting audibly on the length of my skirt or some other detail of my waitressing-mandated appearance. But the more I smiled and flirted, the more I got tipped. And I liked the feeling.

By the time I was 18 years old, I'd progressed from waitressing to working as a promo girl, which demanded a more explicit performance of likeability. I spent my summers offering cheese samples in Waitrose, handing out Nature

Valley bars at Waterloo station, or else circling summer music festivals dressed as a lifeguard and handing out Tic Tacs from a Tic Tac belt strapped around my waist. 'Hey, you look like you need a refreshment. Try a Tic Tac!' I'd say to young boys and girls so high they could hardly register the lurid yellow monstrosity standing before them, nor the outstretched hand offering them the hollow revival of a small sweet. Scattered amongst my product sampling shifts was an evening gig that involved selling cigarettes in nightclubs.

Before you judge me too harshly for this particular job, know that it was hardly my proudest hour, particularly as someone who has never smoked. But I was young and dumb and enticed by the £10-per-hour pay check. So while many of my fellow university politics students spent their summers doing unpaid internships with their local MP or volunteering at charities, I was marching around nightclubs with a pair of neon-pink 'shutter shades' perched on my head (a mandatory part of our uniform) and a tray of cigarettes hanging from my neck, trying to earn some cash. My shift would start at 10pm and alongside another girl around my age, we'd drive around London with a 'chaperone' (a 40-year-old man who turned out to be her boyfriend), dropping into a long list of thumping nightclubs trying to sell our wares. We were instructed to wear a short black dress, high heels and a full face of makeup.

We only took cash, inputting every sale into a mini-pre-iPad-iPad that constantly malfunctioned and messed up our sales records. We'd both keep a manual record of every pack sold for safekeeping, and as we drove home at 4am once the clubs had all shut, we'd cross-check our numbers in the back of the car. If there were any inconsistencies between the system register and our own sales tally, the money would be docked from our pay check.

It wasn't hard to sell cigarettes to drunk people clubbing on a Friday and Saturday night, particularly given that a pack of Camel Blues still cost around £6 then. But I quickly became the highest-selling cigarette girl amongst the army of stock-image, male-gaze blondes deployed on this frightful mission by relying on the very same desire-me charm I'd perfected waiting tables. But the dynamic in this role was slightly different – or rather, the undercurrent to every transaction was more explicit. The men we sold to, because it was mainly men who bought from us as I am sure you're unsurprised to hear, spoke to us like *we* were for sale rather than the cigarettes we were flogging. Their money bought our time, and we represented to them one thing: sex. Or the possibility of it. A pattern became clear after several weeks on the job: the more expensive the nightclub, the higher the tips; the higher the tips, the more entitled our purchasers felt to our time, to our bodies, to the knowledge of our sexual proclivities.

And so the unspoken agreements that framed the performance of my desirability were, in these nightclubs, rendered overt. No more so than when, one evening, a man grabbed my bum before trying to slide his hand up my skirt. I turned to him in protest, shouting, 'You can't do that!' He laughed, drunkenly spitting through his teeth: 'I can touch you however and wherever I want.' My stomach clenched in shame. My dress was short, my lipstick bright, and I'd been intentionally alluring to everyone I spoke to in the hopes they'd buy what I was selling. I meant the cigarettes, but they read: her body. Were they wrong?

In her 2025 memoir of voluntary celibacy, *The Dry Season*, author Melissa Febos describes how she honed her own craft in the power of seduction while waiting tables. The trick, she writes, was to 'render the plates of food a symbol for something else, to exude an air of slight withholding, a little smug but available.' As she approached every table, she had to summon within herself a specific feeling: that she had something they wanted and which she wanted to give, just not yet. It was a fine balance. Seduce too hard and she'd be propositioned by her customer on the spot. Not hard enough, and they'd fail to notice her at all, leaving an insignificant tip on their departure. And then there was the ever-present risk of humiliation – 'the flipside of seduction' for every woman bartering with her body. The object of your seduction might not play ball, which in her case meant they might exploit her flirtation, behaving cruelly in the process and then leave nothing in the way of a tip behind. In my case, they'd take too literally the premise of what I was offering, reaching for my body instead of my cigarettes.

The skills Febos cultivated in cafes across America became the talents that later underpinned her work as a professional dominatrix. Except, she says, in the context of sex work, 'the subtext of my seductive transactions became text. Before I worked with any client, we had a consultation in which he told me exactly what he wanted and I agreed to it or didn't.' Working in a dungeon, there was no song and dance around what was or was not on sale; here the terms and conditions were clear and the offer of sex, in some form or another, was plainly on the table. That and, regardless of how the session went, she was paid well for her time. Whether overtly or not, women are often conditioned to use their sexuality as a bargaining chip for doing business. Be palatable, yes, but better yet? Be fuckable. In sex work, you are just guaranteed to be paid for your powers of seduction.

I thought about all the women founders I read about who are sexually harassed while trying to raise money for their companies. According to one study reported in Forbes,[20] 40% of women founders said they were harassed, with 75% of these reporting unwanted physical contact and 50% saying they'd been propositioned for sex in exchange for funding or contacts. I have never been propositioned so flagrantly in my adult professional life, but when I first started going to job interviews and doing placements after my Master's, my mum would remind me constantly to make sure I looked good. Be glamorous. Look delightful. Resemble someone they (men?) would want in the office. Her message was clear: the better you look, the more likely they are to want you (for the job?).

## Am I a pig or a woman?

French philosopher Jean-Paul Sartre wrote in *Being and Nothingness* (1943) that we become conscious of our body when we are looked on by another, when our body becomes a 'body for others'. For women, this bodily awareness is forged through a particularly violent kind of social objectification. Even before we are touched, we are devoured by hungry eyes, trained to believe that our flesh is a meal to which men are entitled. Or, as Simone de Beauvoir writes in *The Second Sex* (1949), women are always defined in relation to men, reduced to objects of exchange and evaluation, our worth tethered to a sexual economy we didn't create but in which we must participate. 'While he [the man] is not in reference to her; she is the inessential in front of the essential.' From infancy, she is trained to attract, to please, to be useful, to be *desired*. What Melissa Febos made explicit in her transition to sex work, turning subtext into contract, is what most women are taught to perform without terms or boundaries: a sexual availability that lubricates the economy of heterosexual life. Which begs the question: can a woman ever know what she truly desires while living under patriarchy? Could I?

Writing in the 1970s, radical feminist Andrea Dworkin argued no. Men have written the terms and conditions of our sexual economy for thousands of years, she said, establishing a male sexual model within which there can be no true equality. 'They own the sex act', she wrote, 'the language which describes sex, the woman whom they objectify. Men have written the scenario for any sexual fantasy you have ever had or sexual act you have ever engaged in.'[21] Whatever desires we may possess are thus products of our male-centric conditioning – articulations of a male sexual sensibility that is inherently objectifying, aggressive and competitive. Any attempt at engendering equality within this model, which I suppose means any attempt at tackling the orgasm gap or encouraging a 'more clit, less dick'-focused approach to intimacy is, Dworkin concluded, futile. Because it only ever reproduces the male sex model, instead of dismantling it. And it *needs* to be dismantled.

I wonder what Dworkin would have made of porn creator Bonnie Blue. She recently made headlines with a publicity spree claiming she had slept with more than 1,000 men, having built an audience filming herself cruising university towns in search of 'barely legal' boys to feature on her Fansly account (she was recently banned from OnlyFans). Dworkin was of course virulently anti-porn, which she deemed the 'perfect preparation for rape' and framed as a civil rights violation against women. But I wonder how she'd have seen Bonnie? Perhaps as the perfect embodiment of our hyper-individualised, male-centric sexual economy? An exaggerated spectacle bringing to the surface the very subtext of the male sex model she spent her life protesting? Maybe.

Dworkin's writing gave me a new lens through which to review my own experiences of sex. The performativity. The disconnection. The disillusionment in the face of desire. The stitch-up of the subtext. But while the end-point of her theory may be compellingly radical: fuck men (metaphorically NOT literally), it's hard to imagine a scenario whereby I left sex therapy committed to political lesbianism – however attractive a prospect that is becoming in today's dating climate. Does that make me a bad feminist? Perhaps. But there is something inherently disempowering, or maybe just depressing, in a framework that precludes the possibility of pleasure for women *within* today's sexual economy, however problematic it may be. Doubtless my desires have been cultivated in the crucible of patriarchy, but surely there is a way through which I can begin to return to my body from this position of disembodied bystander?

'I feel more like an observer than a participant when I'm having sex,' I tell Aleks. 'As if I'm watching someone else go through the motions of moaning, moving and repositioning. But I'm not really there. I'm not really *in* my body.

'I had a similar feeling the other day while I was standing in front of the mirror. I looked at my reflection almost as though it wasn't mine. Like I couldn't decide which lens I was viewing myself through. Was it the lens of the media, which is forever convincing me to see my body in terms of a trend that must be followed? The eating disorder, which has fuelled the barrage of cruel criticism I've directed at its every curve and contour for as long as I can remember? Or perhaps today I'm seeing myself through the eyes of the man I slept with not long ago, who never called me back? Or maybe the man who wolf-whistled me yesterday while I was walking to work?

'Staring at my reflection, I had all of these competing feelings: *I hate my body. I love my body. I am so very grateful for my body. I feel ugly, sexy, fat* . . . Then I just thought: *Whose body is this?*'

When I was doing my Master's in psychosocial studies (a lofty blend of psychoanalysis, critical/political theory and sociology), we studied a book called *Pig Tales* (translated from the original 1996 French title, *Truismes*) by Marie Derrieussecq. It was part of a gender studies module, and the teacher set this particular text so that we could gather the following week to discuss the module's central topic: objectification. I remember reading the book in one sitting, camped out in our university library with a highlighter in one hand and a pen in the other, furiously taking notes. I was going through the second wind of my feminist awakening at the time, and the book left a deep impression on me, conjuring lucidly on the page the mind–body dissonance I was growing increasingly, personally, cognisant of but could little put into words.

The story follows a woman in a brutally misogynistic world who takes a job at a beauty parlour, where her manager enjoys fondling her breasts and the staff are expected to offer 'extra' services to male clients. She recounts this relentless degradation with breezy indifference, seeming almost to welcome male validation regardless of the form in which it comes. But her body tells another story: she begins to transform into a pig, swelling in size, sprouting bristles, growing extra nipples. Mildly bemused, she adjusts to her hybrid state of woman and swine as those around her respond with unsettling admiration. The tale becomes a grotesque satire of literal objectification, in which women are treated as animals, all while men reveal themselves to be the true pigs.

Reading *Pig Tales*, I recognised what Dworkin meant by a 'male sexual economy'. Rather than resist the daily humiliation of objectification, the protagonist learns instead to live in the body patriarchy has proscribed for her, even as it mutates beyond recognition. *So,* I thought, as I turned through its pages, *am I a pig or a woman? And how would I even know?*

It was around 2014 at the time, meaning we were still several years ahead of activist Tarana Burke's #MeToo movement going viral. Without the language of consent and abuse that the popularisation of #MeToo handed to us, I had yet to put into words experiences that still echoed around the darkest chambers of my mind, even as I felt how they framed the disconnect I experienced from my body. One such experience came suddenly into focus.

It was the penultimate day before the Christmas holidays, and my friend and I were prematurely celebrating at a party being held in a nearby pub. We were both 17 at the time and, after drinking until last orders, we welcomed the invitation to head back with a group of guys to continue the festive celebrations. We had a penchant for boys in bands who were covered in tattoos and averse to showering, so we followed gratefully behind their plumes of cigarette smoke and unwashed hair. They offered us drugs, which we gladly accepted, and as the music blared we danced with abandon, relishing being the only girls in this group of men we so idolised.

As the night turned to early morning, things grew hazy. Eventually, I passed out in a bed somewhere in the house-cum-squat.

The next morning, I woke up groggy, trying to piece together fragments of an evening I could scarcely remember. I had flashbacks of someone kissing me, but I couldn't work out when or where or who. I walked downstairs into the smoky living room, where the boys in bands were still congregating, sprawled across two giant sofas, chain-smoking and drinking whatever dregs remained from the night before. They laughed at me as I walked in and started clapping. 'You had sex with Pete,' they leered. I looked across at the mute painter twice my age, who sat crouched in the corner, his face turned away from the group. We had barely exchanged a single word. I didn't know him at all. My confusion curdled into shame.

I ran upstairs to wake my still-sleeping friend. Did she have any memory of what'd happened? I asked. Reaching for a glass of water next to her bed, she propped herself up, eyes still half closed, and explained what she could remember. She'd walked into the room I was sleeping in and found the mute painter undressing me silently as I lay there unconscious. She and another boy-in-a-band drunkenly pushed him off and carried me out to a sofa on the landing, before heading back downstairs.

My head thrummed with questions. 'Then why did I wake

up back in the bed,' I asked, 'wearing just my knickers?' She shook her head and shrugged.

It was the final day of term and, not wanting to miss the carol concert, I grabbed my bag and coat from downstairs to get the bus to school. Still drunk, I arrived in the sixth-form common room and burst into tears, incoherently trying to explain to a friend what I think maybe, could have, perhaps, potentially have happened. That night at home I sat in the shower scrubbing my skin as hard as I could, trying to rub off whatever part of him remained on me.

I didn't speak about that evening again until sometime in November 2017, when, over dinner in New York, a friend and I began sharing recollections from the past we were now beginning to make sense of. I was angry at myself for not having said anything at the time, I told her. Angrier still that I continued to hang out with those guys, especially that I went back to their house just one week later, as though nothing had happened. And even worse, as though whatever had happened was somehow OK. When my friend who'd been there that night got drunk and said to the leering men, 'Your friend raped my friend,' I shrivelled inside, more so when they responded with outrage, telling her she was lying and to get out of their house. I wished I'd been the type of girl who spoke up, who pushed men away in the face of their unwanted gropes, who called out big and small acts of violence alike, instead of learning simply to tolerate them. But, at 17, I had just wanted men to like me. I had wanted their approval more than I'd craved their respect, no matter the cost to my own body or boundaries. Perhaps I was a pig. Naively acquiescent in the face of my own objectification.

Aleks looks up from her notepad.

'This sense of bodily alienation, as you describe it,' she responds. 'How do you think it might be affecting your relationship to sex?'

'It makes me feel like I am outside of myself when I'm having sex with someone. Almost like I'm not really there. I've felt like that for most of my sexually active life, so I don't really know what I actually want during sex. I just go along with whatever the person I'm with wants.

'Am I enjoying myself? Sometimes. But often, I'm actually taking comfort in the fact I can disconnect. In my ability to step out of my body and jump into a pocket in my head where I feel safe and almost numb.'

I describe to Aleks how this feeling of 'spectatoring' is worst during one-night stands, when the anonymity further fuels my perceived need to perform.

'Afterwards, I feel scooped out. Like my body was just a vessel for fulfilling someone else's needs, ready to be discarded as soon as it's over.

'God. This sounds terrible . . .' I trail off. 'It's not a particularly *empowered* way of having sex, is it?'

Aleks looks at me, pen in hand.

'It's totally OK to enjoy all types of sex,' she responds. 'It's also OK to withdraw your consent during sex. You can ask someone to stop, you know? It sounds as though you step outside of yourself at the point at which it's no longer good for you. But you should be able to stop rather than endure it from some disconnected vantage point. Good sex is dependent on communication before, during and after, right?

'This comes up often among my clients,' she adds. 'A lot of what you're describing is internalised misogyny, and I hear iterations of it all the time. Women become used to seeing themselves through the male gaze and prioritising a man's pleasure so much that they subordinate their own needs to their sexual partners' without thinking – often because, as you've described, they're not even sure what those needs are. This is really common among women.

'OK, I want to give you a piece of homework,' Aleks says, bringing our session to a close. 'I want you to start keeping a pleasure journal.'

Every day I was to keep a list of 3–5 things that brought me pleasure in my body *outside* of a sexual context. The feeling of hot water trickling down my back in the shower. A hot cup of coffee first thing in the morning. The smell of fresh flowers . . . anything. I was to keep a note of whatever felt sensorily good, and really try to take stock of that experience, that pleasure. The point, she explained, was to get me connecting to my body in a sensory way, all while describing these sensations using neutral, non-judgemental language. This would take me away from the usual punitive vocabulary I typically used in relation to my body and create new neural pathways that would get me thinking about it differently. That, she said, is 'a transferable skill we can then apply to sex.'

The following morning, I sipped a mug of hot tea in bed and closed my eyes, allowing the warm liquid to wash over my tongue in what I imagined to be a highly connected, verging on sensual way. I thought about the flavours that tingled across my taste buds, taking note of the warmth spreading down my body with every mouthful. And then I began to paint a picture of what a woman at home in her body and connected to her sensuality might look like. How she would move her body. How she would inhabit every room she entered with purpose and poise, proud to take up space. Uncompromising. How she'd lay claim to her desires with a sense of authority rather than shame. And then fuck with an animalistic hunger for pleasure, disregarding how she looks as she prioritises how she feels and gives voice to what she needs.

*I want to be her*, I thought, taking another sip of tea.

## Chapter 4

# In pursuit of self-pleasure

## The ideology of masturbation

I used to describe the conversations we had during my Master's as intellectual masturbation at its best. However much I enjoyed inserting words like *postulate* and *heuristic* into our classroom discussions, out in the real world people cared little for the sort of detailed, poststructuralist analysis we laboured over in our ivory tower. Like sexual masturbation, intellectual masturbation felt excessive. A self-indulgent exercise that belonged to the bourgeois elite we were otherwise happy to critique through our (champagne) socialist-veering lens. But while I worried these academic conversations were a questionable use of time, or at least I worried other people thought they were, masturbation, of the self-touching variety, was not just wasteful; it was sinful.

I don't remember exactly when this message was first

implanted in my mind, because I don't remember ever having any conversation at all about self-pleasure. Boys wanked, but did girls touch themselves? I'd never considered it. I don't even think I knew about the clit, with its 10,000 nerve endings crying out to be stimulated, until I was late into my teens. I got the hint there might be something worth engaging with down there when I first discovered the particularly pleasant sensation of placing the shower head between my legs while in the bath. I was 11 years old. I held it there by accident at first, and then pretended to continue holding it there by accident because I was concerned about what that nice feeling meant. Did it make me a slut? In God's eyes it did, I was sure. And he was always watching. I stopped myself from going any further with my shower-head experiment and quickly got out of the bath, imagining how he might smite me the following day because of what I'd done. What that was, I wasn't quite sure. But I knew it was bad.

In an essay for the *LA Review of Books* writer Jonathan Alexander critiques the ideology of masturbation in a heteronormative and homophobic society[22]. His own shame and internalised homophobia made self-pleasure difficult, he said. So when he was aroused, alone, he could do little more than rub himself through his boxers, fuck the bed sheets, hump the carpet. He could not touch his penis directly. 'I was already unclean enough,' he wrote, 'having thoughts about other boys. To touch myself directly, hand on my penis, would seem too much like an admission that I was the agent of these desires, as opposed to their victim.' I too sought to disavow my desires because they made me feel dirty. Not only was God always watching and anything insinuating sex a sin, but the very act of placing my hand physically on my vulva felt too overt an admission of lust.

Besides, I didn't know how to desire; I only knew how to be desired. I was comfortable being passive – a receptacle for someone else's pleasure – but the prospect of being active in the pursuit of my own made me uncomfortable. As existentialists Beauvoir and Sartre argued, we become who we are through what we choose. There is no fixed self underneath it all, only the one revealed through our actions and commitments. Like Alexander, I was scared of what my desires revealed about me. I was scared they marked me out as 'promiscuous' of mind and soon of body. And like Aisha, I worried pleasure would tip into excess. The two were inter-changeable in my mind. Best not to open Pandora's Box.

This reticence shifted when, in my second year of university, a friend bought me my first vibrator from Ann Summers. A small, silver bullet she said would change my life. She was surprised I'd never properly wanked before and took it upon herself to rectify that. I felt embarrassed slinking under the duvet covers to hold this small, vibrating object against my clit. More so the idea that my university boyfriend might ever find out. The notion of having a private pocket of intimacy outside of the four walls of our relationship felt suspect. Like eating the forbidden fruit. But the bullet felt good. Perhaps not life-changing, but pleasant enough to keep going back for more. Sometimes I watched porn on my laptop to get me more in the mood. I turned the volume down to zero so my flatmates couldn't hear, and then slammed the screen shut as soon as I'd come, feeling swallowed up by guilt. And still, I didn't ever touch myself with my bare hands. That was too personal an act of intimacy to cultivate with myself.

In the years that followed The Break-Up with my university boyfriend, many of the men I slept with asked that I touch myself while we had sex. In part because it turned them on, but more I suspect because they weren't sure how to do it themselves. They assumed, I suppose, that I was withholding some vital information or technique that would draw from my body an orgasm. But I was as much a stranger to my genitalia as they were. Moreover, it felt horribly exposing to masturbate in front of an audience, even an audience of one. It was like cutting your nails in public. Or flossing on the Tube.

During my second, perhaps third, session with Aleks, the topic of self-pleasure came up. I told her I had a bullet I rarely used and felt weird about touching my own body. I didn't like seeing myself naked, for starters, and it felt like a waste of time. It made me feel dirty. Shame, I said, stood between me and my body.

She was unsurprised to hear this, as she was most of my admissions of perceived sexual deficiency.

'Shame is the most powerful tool for policing sexuality,' Aleks responded.

'The function of shame as an emotion is to encourage us

to connect with our tribe and prompt us to avoid behaviours that might get us "excluded" from the clan. Shame is how a culture enforces its values and the way in which these values subsequently become a part of people's sense of self. We internalise certain norms and then police ourselves and our actions in order to avoid feeling the shame and guilt associated with breaching them.'

Moreover, she continued, shame doesn't just affect the person feeling it; it teaches onlookers what the group forbids. In other words, shame functions as a public broadcast of 'the rules', nudging observers towards conformity. It's why sexual taboos and double standards can persist even when no one is explicitly enforcing them.

'And obviously these values aren't neutral – they are rooted in patriarchal ideology.'

I thought about de Beauvoir's depiction of the adolescent girl who, she writes, 'learns that as the shamed subject of the Look (aka the male gaze), her sex condemn(s) her to a mutilated and frozen existence.' As young girls are conditioned to see themselves through the eyes of others, she argued, we become both subject (the person living in her body) and object (the thing being seen). And because that gaze is sexualised and moralised, we internalise shame: we monitor ourselves – how we dress, sit, move, speak – to avoid provoking judgement or desire. The phrase 'a mutilated and frozen existence' describes what happens to the adolescent girl's inner life as a result. 'Mutilated' because parts of herself (her desire, spontaneity, sensuality) are cut off or suppressed;

'frozen' because she becomes immobilised by self-surveillance. Instead of freely inhabiting her body, she watches it, manages it, and disciplines it. I didn't want to be mutilated or frozen. I wanted to be free.

I'm going to set you a task, Aleks said. 'I want you to seduce yourself.'

To seduce myself?

'Yes. I want you to dedicate an evening to self-pleasure, as if you're going on a date and you're leading up to sex. Light candles. Have a bath. Play music. Spend time dropping into your body in a sensual way. Connecting with all your sensations before using your vibrator. I want you to be really present in the experience.'

I agreed.

Then I went out in search of inspiration. Of the non-porn variety.

## Sex for one

'I packed a bag of sex toys along with a carousel of one hundred colour slides of female genitals and took off across the country to teach sex to feminists.

'At the time it seemed very simple. I'd show them the wide variety of women's sex organs so we'd stop thinking our own were ugly or deformed, and then I'd teach them how to have orgasms by masturbating . . .'

So begins the foreword to Betty Dodson's *Sex For One*, a memoir/masturbation manual which argues that a woman's capacity to achieve orgasm independent of a man is the cornerstone of her liberation.

I discovered Dodson through Hollywood's connoisseur of pleasure paraphernalia, Gwyneth Paltrow – specifically, her Netflix series *The Goop Lab*. And it was there that I was introduced to the guru of self-pleasure – the woman who would inadvertently persuade me to use a carrot in place of a dildo in a moment of masturbatory desperation one Christmas to come.

During her appearance on *The Goop Lab* in 2020, Dodson gave a hint of what years of aiding women in their self-pleasure journeys may have looked like for her, guiding business partner Carlin Ross (the CEO of their company, Dodson and Ross) through a vulva self-examination. It's a practice Dodson has long exhorted every woman to do as a matter of urgency. Lay down a towel, she advises, spread your legs, and with a bright light pointing towards your pubic region, behold the glorious sight of your pussy through the reflection in a well-sized cosmetics mirror. Her rationale? If you don't know what it looks like down there, then you don't know what you're working with when it comes to both self- and partnered pleasure. I whipped out a mirror as soon as the episode was over and, while slightly less enthused by my reflection than Dodson would I'm sure have hoped, it was a revelation, nonetheless.

I quickly fell into a Dodson-shaped research hole, marvelling at the audacity of this sexual savant who was so brazen in extolling the benefits of self-pleasure right up to her death at 91 years old. 'The most consistent sex will be the love affair you have with yourself,' she writes in *Sex for One* (1996). 'Masturbation will get you through childhood, puberty, romance, marriage and divorce, and it will see you through old age.' But it was her 'erotic evolution', as she terms it, during which masturbation became a critical component of her own sexual healing, that so compelled me. More so, her 'feminist commitment' to evangelise her learnings.

Originally from Kansas, Dodson moved to New York when she was 18 years old with just $400 in her pocket, determined to pursue her dreams of becoming a fine artist. After mastering the nude, she moved on to erotic art – paintings of couples having sex and women pleasuring themselves; fine line drawings depicting a variety of vulvas and penises; colourful marker drawings of women in 'goddess pose'. But while her art was alive with sensuality, her personal life was, for a long time, not.

Following ten years in a sexless marriage to advertising executive Frederick Stern, Dodson had a sexual epiphany when, aged 40, she met NYU professor Grant Taylor and was introduced, for the first time, to a vibrator. 'At the time I was sex starved and constantly wanting more sex,' she later wrote, 'especially after he started stimulating my clitoris while we were fucking.' But the real turning point for Dodson was when they started attending, and later hosting, group sex parties, during which Dodson was horrified by how many women – how many otherwise powerful and self-assured women no less – were faking their orgasms. 'Watching men coming while women were pretending was unacceptable to me,'[23] she commented.

But this was the late 60s, and despite the breakthrough in sex research by Masters and Johnson, Freud's shadow still loomed large, fuelling a cultural dismissal of clitoral orgasms while propping up the old male-centric model of sexuality. An essay entitled 'The Myth of the Vaginal Orgasm' (1970) by radical feminist Anne Koedt gives us a sense of the sexual climate at which Dodson was beginning to take aim.

Rebuking Freud for propagating a theory that wasn't based on the study of women's anatomy at all, but rather on 'assumptions of woman as an inferior appendage to man', Koedt criticises Freud's fixation on vaginal orgasms. It was this fixation, she wrote, that was responsible for women faking their orgasms. Women were being taught to blame themselves for not achieving the same level of pleasure as their male counterparts, but they were living in a male-centric sexual paradigm that set them up for failure. 'Looking for a cure to a problem that has none can lead a woman on an endless path of self-hatred and insecurity,' she lamented. 'For she is told by her analyst that not even in her one role allowed in a male society – the role of a woman – is she successful. She is put on the defensive, with phony data as evidence, that she'd better try to be even more feminine . . . That is, shuffle even harder, baby.' Koedt reportedly[24] received death threats following the publication of that seminal piece and soon after left New York, and her feminist activism, behind in pursuit of a 'normal life'.

But Dodson was undeterred. Incensed by the fact so many women around her were being sexually short-changed, she resolved to do something about it.

With the second-wave feminist movement gaining momentum, propelled by consciousness-raising groups where women gathered to share personal experiences of inequality, sex and power, Dodson set about hosting her own gatherings – of a sexual variety, naturally. She began inviting women to her Manhattan apartment, where she'd get everyone to sit around naked as she posed to the group two simple questions: How do you feel about your body? And how do you feel about your orgasm? The format eventually evolved into the *Bodysex* workshops for which she became renowned, which featured group masturbation, genital show-and-tell circles, and frank, uncensored conversations about pleasure.

I got out a pen and promptly added to my list of *Sex Myths*:

- Masturbating is embarrassing
- Masturbating is dirty
- Masturbating is a waste of time

We live and we learn.

For Dodson, masturbation was radical because, she argued, when we are denied the opportunity to create a sexual relationship with ourselves, through culturally imbued ideas of shame and guilt, we're 'easier to manipulate and more accepting of the status quo'. Self-pleasure isn't just about unlocking new bodily sensations – although there is merit alone in that – it is, she wrote, about cultivating an erotic connection to yourself outside of the context of partnered intimacy – one that allows you to get to know your own body (your genitals!) and build sexual self-confidence and knowledge. It is, after all, only when we know what we like, what we don't like, how we want to be touched and what we'd prefer to avoid, that we can communicate clearly with lovers.

Masturbation, she preached, held the key to overcoming the sort of sexual repression that is engendered by a society that continues to equate pleasure with shame. One that propels people to think they're 'frigid' when really they just don't know what they like. 'Sexual skills are like any other skills,' she wrote, 'they're not magically inherited, they have to be learned.'[25]

## Pussy, a reclamation

Towards the end of Jonathan Alexander's essay on masturbation[26], he draws on what he says is a more positive depiction of self-love than the idea which once animated his fraught relationship to self-touch. *Pussy* (2016), an animated short film by Renata Gąsiorowska, tells the story of a young woman attempting to masturbate alone, at home. But her efforts are derailed by a litany of distractions. Her vulva promptly detaches itself from the rest of her body and sets about tackling whatever obstacles are standing in the way of pleasure: a peeping tom from across the courtyard; the woman's own lacklustre touch. However delightful an homage to self-pleasure this short may be, Alexander writes, it emphasises the constant struggle entailed in connecting to one's body. A struggle that requires detachment from both the physical distractions of the outside world, and the mental limitations that hinder us from relaxing into, and exploring, our bodies. Self-pleasure is a *pursuit*, he argues. And, somewhat ironically, given it demands a relative state of relaxation, it needs work.

The first evening I dedicated to self-seduction, I felt like the woman in the film as she struggles to detach from the world in order to connect with her body. I ran myself a bath and lit a candle. Then immediately picked up my phone and started messaging a man who'd recently slid into my DMs. It seemed unlikely we'd meet, but I enjoyed our flirtations and instinctively wanted to bring him in on my night of pleasure. Who needs a peeping tom when you have a digital voyeur forever at your fingertips? To set the sexual scene, I needed male validation. It was hard facing myself naked, alone.

Finally, I forced myself to put away my phone and shut my eyes, allowing the water to wash over me as I sucked in the sweet smell of fig bath oil. I began tentatively touching different parts of myself. Caressing my shins with the same care with which I eventually stroked my boobs, thinking all the while: how did I really want to be touched? After an hour or so in the bath, I dragged myself from the now lukewarm water and went to bed, where I continued to move at that same glacial pace, touching every part of my body before eventually reaching for the vibrator.

It struck me that evening, as it did every other night in which I followed Aleks's instructions and practiced self-seduction, how intentionally I needed to disconnect myself from the busyness of the day. Not to mention the mental chatter filling my mind as a result. It took time. Focus. The *pursuit* of self-pleasure as opposed to an instantaneous relaxation into it. I thought about the dozens of tabs currently open on my laptop and the new productivity planner I'd recently purchased to help better optimise each segment of my day. I thought about the long to-do list I'd updated earlier, which pulled me in multiple directions every morning as I chased the high of being busy, mistaking momentum for progress because I was obsessed with getting ahead. A busy fool. Then I thought about Dodson and her reminder to women that the longest love affair we will ever have is with ourselves. How we neglect so fundamental an erotic connection with our own bodies at our own expense. Pleasure, I reminded myself, is free. It is a bountiful resource we needn't rely on anyone else to provide. How foolhardy I felt to have spent so much time neglecting the most fundamental relationship in my life.

## Sextual pleasure

I recently read[27] that elite athletes often use visualisation as a technique for improving their sporting performance, I told Aleks. By repeatedly imagining you are performing a specific move or exercise in a certain way, research shows you create the same neural pattern in your brain that would occur if the action was actually being performed. 'Mental imagery', the piece noted, 'conditions our minds to react in a certain way so that when the action actually happens, the mind is familiar with how it has to process information, which turns into a better performance for the athlete.' By extension, I wondered, could I (re)train my brain to feel more comfortable during sex by practising over text?

Newly emboldened by my burgeoning relationship to self-pleasure, I'd started texting someone I'd met on an app. Perhaps I was giving off the textual energy of someone deep in the throes of a sexual awakening, because the conversation quickly turned to sex. He asked me what I was into. I said I was trying to figure that out. And then, as though by some tacit agreement, we started to describe in detail exactly what we wanted to do to the other; how we wanted to be touched; where we wanted to go next. While the concept of phone sex had previously made me cringe – more so the idea of getting wet staring at a screen as the other person wanked into the stark blue glow of their device – this familiar stranger was a text-based lothario and self-professed wordsmith. And suddenly, so was I. Flexing a new sexual lexicon I was only now beginning to grow comfortable with.

'Yes,' Aleks replied. 'Or sexting/visualisation can at least help.

'Visualisation is a really powerful tool because it enables you to explore sex in a safe and comfortable environment,' she said, 'thereby allowing you to ground yourself in what is called the parasympathetic nervous system. This brings the body back from the "emergency status" that the *sympathetic* nervous system puts it into. And means that rather than being in fight-or-flight mode, you are in rest-and-digest mode, and better able to experience pleasure.'

When we experience anxiety around sex,[28] she explained, the sympathetic nervous system is activated, which generally makes it harder to relax into your body and experience pleasure. Since I'd learned to associate sex with feelings of shame and insecurity, anxiety was dampening sexual arousal and making it harder to orgasm. The more I worried about not coming, the more anxious I felt and hence the less likely I was to climax. 'Visualisation, or in this case sexting, helps because it allows you to explore sexual fantasies in a safe and relaxed environment (namely, alone in your bedroom), so you can get used to reconnecting with your body as a source of pleasure and experimenting with what you might like sexually.' I blushed at the mental image we might both now be sharing of me alone, at home under the covers, texting and wanking furiously as my nervous system remained in a state of relative calm.

Two months later, the screenwriter and I met for a drink. He was awkward and less sure of himself in the flesh, fidgeting with the coaster beneath his G&T as he mumbled about his various work projects and upcoming travels. But after months establishing a pseudo-sordid intimacy and basking in an intoxicating mix of proximity and longing, familiarity and distance, I felt more invested than I knew I should. We eventually went back to mine, and, after joining my flatmate and her date for a few drinks in the kitchen, we went up to my room. The problem, I quickly learned, with outlining every delicious fantasy you imagine yourself fulfilling with a person from the internet, is that it creates a pretty confronting checklist of sexual items you then feel painfully aware of *not* ticking off should you actually have sex with them. Text-based romances seldom read well off the digital page, and this was no exception. Where communication during sex was, he'd said during one particularly steamy exchange, of utmost importance to him, now he remained silent as he thrust into me repeatedly – his face furrowed in concentration. I waited for it to be over while vowing to myself that the next time I had sex with someone, it would be different. *I* would be different.

Eventually he groaned and rolled off, letting out a satisfied exhale as though he'd just completed a particularly challenging flight of stairs, before falling asleep.

There is nothing more intimate than sleeping next to someone, Milan Kundera notes in *The Unbearable Lightness of Being* (1984). While 'love does not make itself felt in the desire for copulation', he wrote, it does so in the 'desire for shared sleep'. It follows, then, that in the absence of love, or even a base level of affection, sleeping next to a virtual stranger is an unnaturally uncomfortable thing to do and keeps you on sleep-hindering high alert. One study refers to this as the 'first-night effect'. When humans attempt to sleep in new environments or next to new people, one hemisphere of our brain remains more alert, resulting in lighter sleep and greater responsiveness to stimuli. It's like the body's built-in security system going into overdrive, trying to ensure that this stranger doesn't kill us in the night. Lying next to the snoring writer, I felt proof of that theory. I stared at the ceiling, willing the morning to arrive early so I could ask him to leave. Every nerve in my body felt as though it was on end and his unfamiliar smell was making me queasy and claustrophobic in my own bed. Finally, the alarm on his phone went off around 9am and, bleary-eyed, he mumbled about having to be somewhere for a fitting. Something about a wedding and a tux and a friend he hadn't seen for a while. I nodded as relief flooded through my body, ceremoniously bolting the front door as soon as he'd left. I lit a candle and began sage-ing my room.

That afternoon, my flatmate texted me a series of screenshots. The snoring writer had slipped into her DMs ten minutes after he'd left our flat, presumably while still in his cab home, asking what she was doing that night. He had sensed a deep connection between them at our kitchen table and wondered aloud whether she'd felt the same. Did she want to meet that evening to find out?

I wondered what lesson from the social pact this particular shaming was supposed to teach me. Perhaps it was a warning from a god I no longer believed in that trouble was on my newly sexed-up horizon? Or maybe it was a reflection on just how bad at sex I really was? My mind whirred as my body burned with humiliation.

The thing to remember, a friend counselled on the phone

as I walked her through the details, is that we give these strangers who walk off of dating apps and into our lives so much undue power. Before we truly know them, before we've established our boundaries, before we've even properly ascertained whether they're worthy of our time, we hand them the keys to our heart or our body in the wild hope that they'll use them wisely. Just doing it for *the plot*, we reassure ourselves. All the while crumbling every time we have to pick ourselves back up when we're left disappointed or, worse, humiliated. Don't give him that power. He didn't earn it. He doesn't deserve it. He doesn't get to make you feel ashamed.

## Chapter 5

# Dismantle the sex myths that fuck you

## Rewild your garden of sexuality

'I've been keeping a list,' I tell Aleks, 'of all the sex myths I've been compelled to question over the course of our sessions.'

The list had, by this point, grown long, and it was far more expansive than I'd imagined it would become when I first put pen to paper. I started, I told Aleks, with the myths that were directly related to sex – that it's shameful, that it's something we shouldn't talk about, that it's a performance for somebody else's pleasure. Then I moved on to all the niggling points of shame that shaped how I saw self-pleasure.

And then, I just kept on writing, jotting down all the baked-in assumptions around what it means to be a woman, a *good* woman no less, which I'd suddenly discovered tucked into the corners and crevices of my every day. How I should date, who I should date, what I should wear, how loudly I should speak, how self-conscious I should be about the current state of my pubes, how embarrassed I should feel about having sex with someone without showering first, how deferential I should be to the lofty journalist I was currently enamoured by, perceiving him to be better than me in every way simply because he talked about his accolades so very much. And I started to question why I was trying to be liked by every single person I matched with on Hinge, contorting myself into who they wanted me to be even when I could hardly stand them.

'I feel as though I've tugged at a single thread in a ginormous tapestry,' I tell Aleks, 'and while I expected to yank out one long piece of blue yarn, suddenly I'm holding a mass of multicoloured fabric in the palm of my hands. Is this the ground zero of my sexual reawakening . . . ?'

'That's the point of sex therapy,' Aleks informs me. 'It's about deconditioning then reconditioning. And while in this context we're doing this in relation to sex, the process is often applicable to our wider belief system.'

First, she explained, she helps a client identify the belief system that has shaped the way they connect to their body: where have these ideas come from and do they really align with what we want? Then she has to help root out the more deleterious ideas discovered here, along with whatever attendant behaviours may have followed. Ideas like: *my body doesn't deserve pleasure*, accompanied by a reticence towards self-pleasure. Or, *my body is 'broken'*, accompanied by anxiety around sexual intimacy. Or even: *no one will ever find my body attractive*, accompanied by sexual avoidance and a reticence to ever be naked in front of someone. Then comes the process of rebuilding. That is, helping her clients replace all the negative ideas and patterns that have stored up in their sexual consciousness over the years with more positive ones. With ideas that can help people to rebuild trust with their body. She mentions sex educator Emily Nagoski's garden metaphor, which fast becomes my favourite analogy for how we might think about rewriting our sexual story.

In *Come As You Are* (2015), Nagoski writes that on the day you were born you were given a 'new field of rich and fertile soil – the garden of your sexuality'. Instantly, your family and those around you begin planting seeds in this garden, about bodies, gender, sex, pleasure, safety, love. Then your culture steps in and plants a 'variety of weeds and invasive species – windblown seeds of myths about the "ideal sexual person" and ropes of vines about beauty standards, spreading like poison ivy under the fence and over the garden wall'.

Nagoski explains that for some, the lucky ones, their family will help weed out the worst invaders, aka damaging cultural sex myths, and cultivate pleasure-positive ideas instead. But, for many of us, we get stuck with toxic crap that we must eventually spend our adulthood trying to weed out ourselves. While it's frustrating that we have to do this work in our later life, Nagoski also suggests that this process of weeding out the bad stuff is really an opportunity: a chance to create a new sexual landscape entirely on our own terms.

I read *Come As You Are* soon after, while away for the

weekend staying at a friend's house in the countryside. Over long walks through misty fields in muddy boots, said friend and I attempted to describe to one another the current state of our respective sexual gardens. Mine, I admitted, was overrun with ugly weeds, sprouted from the seeds of all the bad ideas around sex I'd internalised growing up and which, through the list I was compiling after every therapy session, I was only now beginning to acknowledge.

'What do you reckon was the first myth you inherited?' my friend asked. 'Like the first poisonous seed in your luscious garden of sexuality?'

I thought about it, trying to disentangle a lifetime of confusing ideas.

'I guess the notion of virginity,' I finally responded. 'It framed how I saw sex: what it meant for me as a girl, who it was for, what it represented societally. And it was also the first sexual concept I unknowingly ever came into contact with.'

I was raised a Christian, so, growing up, I went to church most Sundays with my mum and sister. My dad had a 'private' relationship to God, he told us, which I later discovered meant he was actually an atheist. Nonetheless, he considered our upbringing in the church a net positive and not something worth disputing with my staunchly Christian mother. Pick your battles and all that. So, every week for a not insignificant part of my childhood, I went to church and listened to a priest regale us with stories concerning the miraculous birth of baby Jesus, born, of course, to the teenage 'virgin' Mary. Alongside my fellow churchgoers I was being quietly, casually indoctrinated with ideas about the sanctity of women's virginal purity.

The notion of virginity proved an enduring theme over the years to come, as I explained to my friend, imagining myself back in the sweaty London clubs in which I first became aware of what I represented to men.

## The virginity myth

My best friend Elspeth and I met at around 14 years old in south-east London while shimmying our way into whatever pubs and bars would turn a blind eye to our obviously fake IDs. It was 2006, and we were in the crucible of the Indie-sleaze era, dressed head to toe in varyingly well-to-weirdly put-together ensembles of Rocket vintage and fake fur coats galore. In pursuit of our imagined rockstar lovers, we went out as much as we could, which for me meant as often as my parents could be persuaded that it was indeed an excellent idea to let me 'stay at a friend's house' on a school night. We marvelled at this new realm of London to which our fake IDs had suddenly given us access.

From sticky-floored pubs in New Cross and Peckham, to the pulsating clubs that lit up Soho (and have since all been shut down – here's to Madam Jojo's and Punk), to the self-consciously cool bars of Shoreditch (some of which still stand, self-conscious and cool), we thrilled in the joy of a bouncer saying 'come in' and celebrated each time by drinking as much as we could, as quickly as possible. To be a child was to be trapped in a matrix of rules and homework, early school starts and tyrannical-seeming parents. We wanted to be grownups. And so to the clubs we flocked, children dressed up as adults, basking in the presence of people twice our age. As we pretended to belong, we sought to keep up with the drinking, the drugs and the veneer of London cool. The following morning, if we'd made it out on a weeknight, we'd be back at our school desks by 8am sharp, dizzy from last night's adventure.

How well we pulled off being baby teens parading as young adults, I don't know. But when it came to men, our age didn't matter.

One Thursday evening I was dancing at my favourite club night, Smash and Grab, and relishing the attention of a tall man with dark glasses who had sidled up next to me so we could sway our hips in some sort of unison. I was wearing a leopard-print T-shirt tucked into short shorts and my hair was plaited on top of my head, my face framed by two giant gold hoop earrings. With my fake eyelashes glued on tight and liquid eyeliner drawn out in large wings on either side, I imagined myself like Edie Sedgwick, dancing through The Factory with a cigarette in one hand and a martini in the other, Andy Warhol just a few conversations away. (Let us never forget the unmatched power of teenage delusion.)

As the tall man in glasses got closer, I felt a warm thrill move through my body. He pointed towards the bar and I followed suit. Over one tequila soda after another, he told me about his job in publishing and some impressive professional accolades. I told him I was 18, an aspiring writer interning at a glossy magazine. We snogged, legs entangled. As the evening wore on, I got progressively more drunk and sloppy: a little rag doll being propped up by the 42-year-old 'creative'.

'Do you want to come back to mine?' he eventually whispered in my ear as we continued dancing. By now my vision was a blur and I wanted to find my friends.

'Can I tell you a secret?' I responded conspiratorially. He leant in closer. 'I'm actually 15.'

He looked at me stunned, then straightened up and said he had to go. I was momentarily affronted. *How dare he!* I thought childishly, then went in search of Elspeth. But before I could find her, the gangly professional in his suit jacket and T-shirt was back. He guided me towards the rear end of the club and we started snogging haphazardly against the wall.

'Come back to mine,' he said again.

'But I'm 15,' I replied, half pleased, half taken aback. Surely, he didn't actually want to shag a child?

'Does that mean you're a virgin?' he questioned, pulling his head back and drinking me in.

'Um, yes.'

His eyes lit up and he pulled me closer.

'Come back with me,' he insisted. 'I want you.'

In *Losing It: Sex Education for the 21st Century* (2023), journalist Sophia Smith Galer explores the way specific sex myths disproportionately harm women. Chief among them is the virginity myth. Like me, Sophia grew up with the idea that a woman's 'virginity' was the property of her future husband, except it was a schoolteacher rather than a priest who first instilled in her the supposed value of a woman remaining 'untouched' till marriage. While delivering a sex ed class, said teacher used the rather unfortunate analogy between a woman's virginity and some sort of superglue, Galer writes, warning her class that every time they had sex, they would lose some of their 'special glue'. Eventually, she warned them, it would all be gone.

The virginity myth is often the first sex myth women are conditioned to believe because it is so deeply embedded in our cultural psyche. In the US, for example, 'purity balls' invite young women to pledge chastity until marriage, while fathers vow to protect their daughters' sexual 'innocence'. Abstinence-only sex education reinforces this framing, casting sex outside of marriage as a moral failure or loss. In parts of Europe and the Middle East, the cultural emphasis on virginity has even led to the availability of cosmetic procedures such as hymen reconstruction (hymenorrhaphy), designed to allow women to appear 'virginal' on their wedding night.

Across cultures, virginity has been treated as an anatomical fact – something located in the body, rather than what it actually is: an ideological construct that ties women's sexual behaviour to moral worth. The power of this myth lies, then, in what it establishes. Sex is framed as something men take and women give; something that increases male status while diminishing female value. Religious narratives, from the Virgin Mary onward, reinforce the idea that female virtue is bound to women being sexually untouched. Virginity is thus the ground zero sex myth: the one that teaches women to understand their bodies and desires as existing in service of others, rather than belonging to themselves.

Sophia and I are around the same age, meaning that the cultural backdrop against which we were conditioned around virginity was confusingly hypersexualised. This was the early noughties after all, an era in which tabloid newspapers had giant pictures of topless models on Page Three; the Victoria's Secret fashion show was screened on ABC for the first time (2001), during which host Rupert Everett noted that 'security is tight and so are the girls!'; Britney Spears was sweating in a pink thong over her jeans in a music video for 'Toxic' (2004), and 50 Cent was musing about his 'Candy Shop' and all the delicious things a girl could lick there (2005); the birth of the internet had heralded the growth of online porn (late 90s, early 2000s) and the top shelves of newsagents everywhere were lined with 'lads' mags' displaying scantily clad women with ginormous boobs, an odd accompaniment to the purchase of a 50p bag of sweets.

At 11 years old (2003), I was transfixed by the girls and women I saw on MTV, who epitomised the sexual allure I was being told to both fear and idolise all at once. I danced in front of the TV to music videos I didn't understand the words to and begged my mum to let me buy a bra so I could have the straps on show like all the sexy women I saw on screen. I was desperate to be inducted into the scintillating realm of adulthood that was so accessible to me through TV and later the internet, and yet so frustratingly out of reach from the dull suburbia in which I lived. When finally she relented and allowed me to purchase a trainer bra, which slid above my nipples every time I raised my hand in class, I wore nothing but strap tops for the rest of the summer. This was as close to a version of sexy I felt, at 11, I could achieve.

In *Female Chauvinist Pigs* (2005), Ariel Levy describes this period in the early noughties in terms of the rise of 'raunch culture' – a time in which we had societally determined that 'all empowered women must be overtly and publicly sexual, and because the only sign of sexuality we seem to be able to recognise is a direct allusion to the red-light entertainment, we have laced the sleazy energy and aesthetic of a topless club or a Penthouse shoot throughout our entire culture.' From art to culture to politics, she argues, we witnessed then the pornification of, well, everything. Or as OG *Playboy* bunny Jenna Jameson's publisher, Judith Regan, told CBS in 2005: 'I believe that there is a porno-ization of the culture . . . What that means is that if you watch every single thing that's going on out there in popular culture, you will see females scantily clad, implanted, dressed up like porn stars and so on, and that this is very acceptable.'

Unbeknownst to my angsty pre-teen/teen self, we were living in the twilight zone between the pre- and post-internet age in which the introduction of AOL dial-up was about to open up a whole new realm to me and my friends, giving us what at first felt like a telescope with which to view the outside world, and later a drawbridge, inviting us fully in. And unlike analogue magazines and newspapers, this was an arena we could peruse outside the watchful eye of our parents. In the internet world we were free to roam, to talk to strangers on Habbo Hotel and attempt to decode their sexual shorthands; to chat to boys on MSN Messenger and convince them we knew whatever sex act they referenced all while revealing that 'yes!', we were indeed wearing pink thongs, despite being forbidden by our mums to buy any. The internet gave us a space in which we as children could anonymously appropriate the lexicon of adult sexual culture, all while soaking up even more of it in chat rooms, on gossip sites and eventually through social media. Once again, we were being primed to perform our sexuality rather than own it.

## The cautionary tale of Britney Spears

It was around the time of the trainer bra that the notion of virginity first took on some semblance of cultural significance to me outside of the context of the Virgin Mary and my OFF-LIMITS, SEX ED folder from primary school RSHE. My dad had decided to take me and my younger sister (eight years old) to see Britney Spears's new film *Crossroads* (2012) as a weekend treat. He obviously hadn't read up on the movie beforehand, since the entire plot was centred around Britney losing her virginity.

Looking back on *Crossroads*, which was written by none other than a pre-fame Shonda Rhimes, over 20 years on from its release, this focus on Britney's 'virginity' takes on a renewed significance. The early noughties were a particularly toxic time for women in the public eye, hounded as they were by a savage media circus navigating the fresh hinterland of the internet. Spears was among the most cruelly targeted of the young celebs whose lives ended up publicly straddling the two worlds I was similarly learning to navigate: pre- and post-internet. As a teenager, she was pushed into the internet fish tank so that her evolution from teen singer to world-famous popstar was scrutinised within an inch of its life by a tabloid press that was hungry for ever more salacious, clickbait content. Nothing was obsessed over more doggedly than her sexual status. And it was something she – or, rather, her marketing team – played into.

The quintessential good girl next door, Britney wore a purity ring on her finger signifying that she was 'saving herself' until marriage. Her early pop persona was premised on her being sweet and virginal, a schoolgirl in bunches who wrote lesson notes with a fluffy pink pen while blowing bubble gum. But there was a Lolita-esque quality in the performativity of her innocence, so insouciantly accompanied by her direct appeal to the male gaze. Short skirts, long socks and a bra on show. Her virginity was offered up provocatively with a 'look don't touch' sleight of hand. Because isn't that really what our obsession with virginity is anyway? A vehicle through which we can fixate on a singular image of female sexuality as an object for male consumption? A way of offering the promise of sex to every man (could it be you on whom she bestows her *special gift*?), the value of which is maintained only by there being no actual sex. 'The young girl's purity allows hope for every kind of licence,' writes Simone De Beauvoir in *The Second Sex* (1949), 'and no one knows what perversities are concealed in her innocence. Neither child nor adult, the virgin is one of the privileged exponents of feminine mystery . . .'

As author Sarah Ditum explores in her book *Toxic: Women, Fame and The Noughties* (2024), Britney's virginity became so highly prized a cultural commodity that one 'mystery businessman' allegedly approached her record label offering to buy it for a cool sum of £7.5 million[29] (equivalent to £13 million today). It's an odd thought, that someone might peg so high a value on, what? On knowing that he is the first one to enter a young girl? Knowing that as soon as he's done so, by virginity myth standards, she will have 'lost' something? That she will no longer be the same again, that she is now impure, worth less, tarred by the legacy of S.E.X.?

At its core, then, the virginity myth is the eternal expectation that has been foisted upon women from time immemorial: that our sexuality, our bodies, our desires are designed for another's consumption, never for our own pleasure. The stories change, but the message stays the same: you must be sexy for a man, but you must not enjoy your sexuality for yourself.

When Justin and Britney eventually broke up in 2002 after nearly three years of dating, Justin released the music video for 'Cry Me a River', which insinuated Britney had cheated on him. It starred a Britney doppelganger playing the woman who breaks his heart. In her 2024 memoir *The*

*Woman In Me*, Britney notes how the media fallout from the video painted her as 'a harlot who'd broken the heart of America's golden boy', when really, she writes: 'I was comatose in Louisiana, and he was happily running around Hollywood.' She was offered up as the cautionary tale for what happens to the fallen woman. But Britney also writes that she felt relieved when Justin admitted to the world they'd had sex, even if it seemed an act of self-promotional deceit at the time. 'Was I mad at being "outed" by him as sexually active? No. I liked that Justin did that.' Admitting that she 'lost her virginity' at the age of 14, she writes that she never understood why her team was so adamant about portraying her as an 'eternal virgin'. I'd hazard a guess it was just good business.

Five years later, the world was awash with images of Britney shaving her head. Reports suggest she walked into the salon in California demanding a buzz cut and, when the salon owner refused, grabbed a pair of clippers and did it herself, all while the paparazzi continued snapping away through the window. 'I don't want anyone touching me. I'm tired of everyone touching me,' she said. The world had feasted upon her body for too long and she was taking back control of her image – desexualising herself and removing an emblem of female attractiveness. No longer the Barbie-doll blonde, her shaven head became the symbol of her break from the patriarchal contract that had been thrust upon her since childhood. The sad irony being that these images circulated just one year before she was placed under a conservatorship and became, to all intents and purposes, the property of her father, James P. Spears. Once again, a cautionary tale to all women who dare to refuse the performance of femininity as it is mandated by the patriarchy.

Losing one's 'virginity' was a hot topic at my secondary school, not least because I went to an all-girls' school that made us both sexually deprived and boy obsessed all in one go. I was a Good Christian Girl when I first started at my independent day school, and believed as strongly in the idea that sex should be reserved for marriage as I did in my God-given right to marry Draco Malfoy. All's fair in love and war, after all. Perhaps my penchant for a Slytherin man was a foreshadowing of my eventual proclivity for your stereotypical bad boy? Who's to say? Nonetheless, I considered my status as an untouched virgin an integral part of my Christian identity and looked upon sex as something sacred. I would be deflowered on my wedding day, I vowed, an event I had planned from the age of eight, complete with a meticulously designed monstrosity of a white tulle dress that screamed VIRGIN. Best leave no one guessing. Coupled with my pre-teen nun-like commitment to sexual abstinence, I also decided that I would never drink nor take drugs, nor shoplift. Of course, it didn't take long for me to be corrupted. Blame my religiously rebellious best friend, our overzealous school environment or the general boredom of youth, it matters little, because the facts we're dealing with here concern my inevitable fall from Christian Good Girl Grace . . . sort of.

By age 13, I had been convinced by said rebellious friend to wet my lips – 'just once,' she said! – with a WKD (a sugary blue vodka drink) that I inevitably found so deliriously delicious I went back for more, more, more. Soon we migrated to Glen's vodka, which we purchased from whichever local off-licence chose to believe we were indeed 18, despite all evidence pointing to the contrary. I did once get asked the date of my birthday while attempting to load up on WKDs and made the rookie error of throwing up a date from the 18th century. I promptly scurried out, my head hung in shame.

Lured in by cheap booze and the promise of an early foray into adulthood, we started spending our weekends drinking in the park and trying our damndest to meet boys. But while my ardent religiosity began to wane, my relationship to sex remained complicated, tugged on the one hand by my Christian-informed view that sex was sacred and special, and on the other by the mounting peer pressure that formed as everyone around me began exploring their sexuality with such apparent ease. Given that my first kiss, with a boy my best friend had only recently broken up with (the treachery), was a slobbery, messy affair – one that culminated in him asking 'What was that?', to my deep, deep shame – I had little faith in how naturally I would take to everything intended to follow. All the while, one thing remained certain for me: sex was something that men took and women gave. Something that men were applauded and women judged for. To be a prude or a slut? That was the question.

I didn't go home with the 42-year-old creative because I

was scared. Not because I thought he would hurt me (I was naively oblivious to this obvious potential threat), but because the idea of having sex terrified me. I'd learned how to perform a youthful sort of sex appeal to attract men, but it was provocation without substance. Without any understanding of what it would mean to follow up on the insinuations of sex I placed on the table. At 15, I didn't know my body, but I implicitly understood the value of what I offered to men in being a 'virgin'. I was participating in a power dynamic I didn't understand but was conditioned to play into.

## Fast girl

'Come on, Emma. If you could decide between a partner having slept with 150 people before you, or two, you would always go for two.'

I was having dinner with a close friend and had just relayed to him that I was deep in the throes of a sexual awakening. The revelation intrigued him and prompted a far more in-depth discussion concerning our respective sex lives than we were used to. I was trying to convince him that my recent foray into sexting did indeed mark a *significant* step forward in said awakening and was not to be sniffed at. 'Baby steps!' I kept saying while waving a forkful of steak in his direction. Meanwhile, he was earnestly trying to explain why he had such deep misgivings about his girlfriend's sexual past. Apparently, she'd slept with 'a lot' of men before him. He admitted it seemed hypocritical, given that he'd slept with dozens of women previously, but he didn't like that she seemed so unapologetic about her sexual history. She couldn't admit that her behaviour had been *bad*, he said, and she remained concerningly unrepentant.

I contemplated the toss-up.

Did I, or should I, care about a hypothetical future partner's sexual history? Was it really preferable for them to have a lower 'body count'?

'I don't think I would,' I replied. 'Providing we are on the same page regarding what we both now want and where we stand, exclusivity-wise, I'm not bothered about what they've done before. And actually, I'd probably appreciate a bit of experience and sexual curiosity, if only to help further push me along in this period of sexual rewilding.' My friend looked at me blankly. Clearly, no one had thrust a copy of *Come As You Are* into his hands yet, and he was none the wiser as to just how overrun his own backyard was with toxic sex myths.

I mentioned this conversation to Aleks in our subsequent session. I didn't understand why someone deeply atheistic could also be so moralistic as to sound biblical while condemning his partner's sexual past. He was a generally progressive person. That a man I otherwise cherished could be so brazen in reinforcing the sort of sexual shame I was in this virtual therapy room trying to shed left a bitter taste in my mouth. I thought again about my list of sex myths and how it revealed the ways in which some of the most problematic ideas about sex and bodies and gender are perpetuated.

It was becoming the most concerning part of this list-writing endeavour – recognising all the small ways in which bad ideas are embedded into our collective consciousness and then taken for granted as default.

'Are you familiar with the Madonna–Whore Complex?' Aleks asked. It was an idea popularised by Freud in the 1920s which suggested that men see women in one of two ways: as good, virginal 'Madonnas' who they can marry, or promiscuous, seductive 'whores' they can fuck.

'"Where such men love they have no desire and where they desire they cannot love," Freud said. A woman can either be sexually desirable and erotic or she can be pure and lovable. She cannot be both.'

I felt short-changed.

Years later, I returned to this topic when researching an article. I was curious as to how this reductive binary had affected other women, so I set up a series of interviews with people whose work dissected the topic of sexual shame in one way or another. Among my interviewees was a woman whose job title alone merited an interview: mythologist. She is also a sex educator and author.

Over lunch, Seema Anand explained her own complicated relationship to sex and shame growing up in 1960s Punjab, India. As a teenager, she said, her understanding of sexuality was shaped by two opposing worldviews. On one side, the lingering legacy of Christian doctrine, particularly the idea of 'original sin', which had cast sex as something shameful and guilt-ridden (Christianity was a minority religion in India, but British colonial rule had imported Victorian values about modesty, chastity and female obedience, embedding them in everything from education to the law). On the other, there was the forgotten wisdom of the *Kama Sutra*, an ancient Indian text that framed pleasure as sacred – a vital, even spiritual, part of a well-lived life. Anand's adolescent mind was tugged in both directions: shame or transcendence? Sin or sensuality?

This paradoxical pull made her look upon her body and its capacity for pleasure with fear and suspicion. She didn't want to be considered a 'fast girl' – someone perceived as easy to get into bed. That was the worst insult you could throw at a woman. So she disconnected from her body's desires. When she entered into an arranged marriage at 23, with the man to whom she remains married today at 63, sex became something they did but never discussed.

Often, she said, she felt broken.

She didn't want to tell anyone else how she was feeling because, of course, she felt ashamed. As Brené Brown writes, 'Shame corrodes the very part of us that believes we are capable of change.'[30] It shrinks us, making us feel inadequate, incapable and somehow defective. And so we don't give voice to what's going on, thinking that if we pretend everything's fine then we can at least escape the perceived social isolation that comes with feeling like we're the only ones with a problem. That changed, however, when, during her third pregnancy at age 37, she found herself devouring erotic literature her friends had left by her bedside as a solace for her hormone-induced horniness – books were also the only viable alternative to porn there was then, she said. As she immersed herself in these pleasure-filled stories, it felt like a spark was being lit. And it occurred to her: if she could feel turned on, alone while lying in bed reading a stack of erotic literature, then she wasn't the problem. The sex she was having was the problem. The expectations *surrounding* the sex she was having was the problem. The litany of stories that had for so long shaped the way she'd seen pleasure was the problem.

'I can remember the feeling from so long ago,' she said. 'I felt like Atlas when he shrugged off the boulder.'

And so she started dedicating time to self-pleasure, to getting to know what her body liked and what it didn't. Then she began vocalising these desires in the bedroom, telling her husband what she wanted to explore (to begin with, somewhat unsuccessfully, she admits – he was as surprised by this new version of his wife as she was). Now, she said, 'pleasure has become part of what makes me feel alive, where I feel creative, where I feel happy, where my brain is tingling.

'Pleasure is the difference between apathy and aliveness.'

There is so much power, she concluded, in stories. The stories we tell about ourselves shape the way we see the world and hence our role in it. Stories define our identity. So, if you want to change some element of your life or your mind, you need to rewrite the stories that have shaped it. You can start small, she insisted. 'Look at your life as a series of tiny, tiny stories, and then start to change one ending at a time . . .'

I returned to my list of sex myths and added several new lines.

- If I like sex, I am a slut.
- If I don't want to have sex, I am a prude.
- If I don't like the sex I am having, I am defective.
- My *relationship* to sex, whatever it looks like, is shameful.

I liked thinking about these myths not just as toxic weeds I needed to pluck from my garden, but as individual stories, the endings of which I could change. A mythologist has such extraordinary power, I thought. They follow myths back to their ancient roots as a way of making sense of the world and the belief systems that underpin how we see it. And in so doing, they uncover all the tentacles of the ideas we have come to take for granted as truths. They're like archaeologists, or perhaps translators, exposing the underbelly of different cultures and the power structures they support.

Seema had become fascinated by the power of mythology long before she turned her focus to the stories that had disconnected her from her body and its capacity for pleasure, but as soon as she did, those stories unravelled. Or, at least, the ones that linked sex with shame and pleasure with promiscuity did. And what was left when these ideas – influenced as they were by rigid Christian doctrine, which cast the body as a battleground for temptation and named chastity the highest virtue – were dismantled? The opportunity to rewrite her own sex story by drawing instead on teachings from the *Kama Sutra*, a book that has been historically trivialised as a collection of sex positions. That is in large thanks to its first translator, one Sir Richard Burton, who focused almost exclusively on the sex chapters and hence stoked the Western misconception that the *Kama Sutra* was exclusively a sex manual. But it is perhaps better described, Seema said, as a book exploring the art of pleasure. From foreplay and kissing to the emotional and spiritual dimensions of sex.

I left Seema thinking about the story of shame she'd carried for so much of her life. How for so long she'd been disconnected from her body because she was scared of being branded, to all intents and purposes, a slut. As though 'slut' was a possible, inevitable condition rather than a word invented to separate women from themselves and make us afraid of our own pleasure. I thought about how these stories become internalised. How they become the lens through which we learn to see ourselves and others too. How many women throughout history have been punished for being 'a slut'?

I also felt confronted by our conversation. Faced with a particularly egregious garden weed I realised I needed to rid myself of. When I started sex therapy, I learned that my connection to sex and pleasure was something I could improve. That it wasn't a static thing, nor a statement of fact about who I am or how my body works. Instead, it was something I could nurture and grow. A myriad of new avenues opened. I wondered how I'd make up for all the lost time I'd squandered while at war with my body. I suddenly felt an anxiety I'd only ever associated with my work life: I worried

I was running out of time. How many 'good' years did I have left to explore this new facet of my body I'd hitherto closed off? How much time did I have left to explore my sexuality?

Speaking to Seema, it occurred to me how limited my view of a woman's sexual life was. And how narrow my perception of pleasure, which I had somehow tied to youth. Like it was something available to me only for as long as I was young(ish) and dating and still in my 'prime'. But what is a woman's prime if not the window of perceived opportunity designated by society as the time in which she is of value *to others*. When she is hot and young. Fuckable and impregnatable. But what happens outside of this window of a woman's societally ascribed worth? According to Seema: a lot. I started to interrogate the idea that my sexuality had an expiration date and my pleasure was youth-bound. It struck me that the shame I'd inherited as a girl was not an anomaly, but part of a much older lineage – a long cultural tradition of weaponising women's sexuality against us.

## She's a devil, she's a whore. No, wait, she's a witch!

In my final year of school, we started learning about the witch trials in history class. This represented somewhat of a departure from the rest of our syllabus, which as far as I can remember was largely dominated by the study of kings. Lots and lots of kings. Often waging war. Sometimes beheading their wives. Generally behaving quite badly. Suffice it to say I remember little of what was taught about King Henry VIII or those who followed him, but I do have a somewhat crisper recollection of the women burned during centuries of mass femicide.

In 1485, a man named Heinrich Kramer conducted an infamous witch trial in Innsbruck, Austria, targeting a group of women he accused of having sex with the devil. The local bishop was so appalled[31] by Kramer's fixation on the accused's sex lives, and the aggression with which he interrogated them, that he stopped the trial, dismissed Kramer and released everyone accused. But Kramer, while humiliated, was undeterred, convinced[32] as he was that women's bodies were the vehicle through which the devil worked, their lust his portal into the world. These carnal temptresses must be stopped! He soldiered on.

And so, one year later he published the *Malleus Maleficarum (The Hammer of Witches)*, the now-notorious text that helped justify the persecution of (predominantly) women as witches. In it he detailed why women are more susceptible to witchcraft: because they are 'feebler in both mind and body' and because 'all witchcraft comes from carnal lust, which is in women insatiable.' He also laid out in extensive, almost pornographic, detail the specifically sexual nature of numerous witchcraft crimes: they had sex with demons; they stole men's penises and hid them in nests or boxes; they caused men impotence; they bewitched men into lustful acts, driving them to adultery; they killed unborn children, caused miscarriages and even obstructed conception.

Over more than three centuries, an estimated 110,000 witch trials took place across Europe, with roughly half ending in execution. Of those accused, around 80–85% were women, the majority above the age of 40.[33]

Research[34] suggests older women living at the edge of the village, no longer able to contribute economically to society and thus deemed a 'burden', were most likely to be targeted. But in Kramer's view, every woman's body was suspect. A witch was at once old, ugly and vengeful because she'd lost her looks, or else young and insatiable with lust. She was poor and desperate, or else too opinionated and even knowledgeable. She was barren or else she was the ultimate she-devil of a human: a midwife, responsible for killing babies or offering them up to Satan. In short, any woman who in some way defied patriarchal control could be accused of witchcraft. The seed of my early feminism had been planted.

Centuries later, and the charge of witchcraft is still being levelled against women, specifically older women who dare to raise their heads above the parapet. I was working for Sky News during the 2016 presidential election – a time when Trump still felt like a bad joke dunked in tanning oil and Hillary Clinton a comparatively steady pair of hands. But even as the left ridiculed Trump's 'build the wall' approach to foreign policy, and his red-hat-branded *Make America Great Again* sloganeering, Clinton was being tarred as the Wicked Witch of the Left by her opponents, portrayed on American social media wearing a black hat and riding a broomstick, or else cackling with green skin. Accusations of witchery were revived once again when Kamala Harris ran for President in 2024. One evangelical pastor and pro-Trump figure, Lance Wallnau, went so far as to explicitly accuse her of using 'witchcraft' and an 'occult spirit' to manipulate voters. If only her spells had worked.

While the use of misogynistic slurs was unsurprising, there is something particularly potent about evocations of 'witch!' within a political context. Not least when used in reference to powerful, older women like Harris and Clinton (60 and 69 years old respectively at the time of running for office).

Within a patriarchal paradigm, a woman's value is consistently tied to two things: her fuckability and her impregnatability, meaning her greatest social currency is her youth. When she is no longer desirable to men, and when she is outside her window of fertility, she is depicted as culturally obsolete. We may be centuries on from Kramer's text encouraging femicide, but the logic that underpinned it remains the same. Consider that women over 50 are consistently rated as less electable than men of the same age; that in Hollywood, where 25 is too old to be an ingénue, a leading man's average[35] romantic co-star stays in her twenties no matter how old he gets; that studies[36] show women report feeling 'invisible' around age 45–55 – professionally, personally, sexually. In Sylvia Plath's poem 'Mirror' (1961), she portrays aging as the spectre that haunts the younger woman. Each time she catches her reflection, she sees herself being overtaken by someone older – a version of herself she's been taught to fear.

It is little wonder the 'anti-aging' industry is set to grow to US\$87.11 billion by 2030.[37] Or that women make up around 80% of the revenue base. We are primed to fend off any creeping sign of age. This, after all, is the year in which Lindsay Lohan revealed her new face, visibly reversing the last decade as she stepped onto the global stage taut, dewy and glowing. And we loved her for it. The Redemption Facelift heralded her return to our screens. The years in which she was plastered across tabloids and branded a mess were forgotten because she was back to a state we recognise as inherently good: hot and youthful. The essential attributes for women who are continually reminded that our status in society is tied to our being appealing to, and in service of, men. Men who are deemed to get wiser and more powerful with age, all while women supposedly lose their value. We may not physically burn women at the stake today, but we dispose of them metaphorically all the same.

I contemplated the effects of this cultural erasure of older women a lot last summer, as I read *All Fours* (2024) – Miranda July's deeply erotic novel about a messy, pre-menopausal woman who leaves her husband and young child on the pretence of going on a road trip. Instead of driving across America, she shacks up in a motel on the side of the motorway and has a sort-of affair with a younger man called Davey. They never have sex per se, but he does pull out her bloody tampon while she's perched above his lap on the loo – my favourite and most sensual non-sex sex scene of all time. When eventually our flawed and deeply horny protagonist has a one-night stand with another older woman, Audra (who also happens to be Davey's ex-lover), it hits me that I have seldom, if ever, read anything so erotic concerning women of that age. Typically, women above about 45 are presented as sexless: mothers, grandmothers, stern headmistresses; career-hungry eunuchs. They are rarely the protagonist in any story about sex or desire.

But July's sex-hungry pre-menopausal figure was, I realised, exactly the heroine I craved. Neither Madonna nor Whore, she's simply a horny, complex, sometimes problematic woman in her late forties who wants sex and is unashamed in her pursuit of pleasure. That we do not see more of her strewn across our collective cultural horizon is a stitch-up. A patriarchal ruse of grand proportions. Because the desexualisation and general exclusion of middle-aged women and beyond reinforces women's fear around aging. It makes us afraid of our aging bodies even as we get older and wiser and smarter and more powerful. But what if this next chapter beyond our male-desire-orientated fuckability and heteronormative-coded impregnatability is actually where we find a whole new dimension to our pleasure? A point at which our body no longer belongs to a society hungry for our youth and our beauty, but is finally returned to us? Ours to enjoy and explore outside of the pressures associated with our fertile years? (I say fertile years because even for those who don't want, or can't have, children, women are all too often valued in relation to fertility as it is defined by age.)

That's how Chloe Macintosh, founder of the sexual

wellness app Kama, described the stage of life she is now in at 50 years old – much to her own surprise, given she'd always seen menopause as the 'end of life'. She too subscribed to the myth that getting older as a woman meant losing everything she valued. 'I thought it meant losing sexiness, and sexuality,' she told me. 'That it represented the end of flirting, the end of being seen, the end of everything. I thought you become this sexless person that no one wants around. And that's just so terrible.' Instead, the opposite happened.

## The erotic resistance to the double standard of aging

When I first met Chloe, she was wearing a broad-brimmed hat with a feather perched jauntily on the side, the sartorial staple of Ibizan island-dwellers, I'd recently learned. A chain of small beads formed a layer of delicate armour across her chest. Her skin was tanned, her hair dark, her eyes piercing blue. She spoke in a thick French accent which gave her every word an erotic leverage I could but dream of. In my broad-shouldered cream suit and tightly slicked-back bun, I felt severe in comparison. I had been asked to interview Chloe for an evening discussion at a wellness festival in Ibiza. Over the course of our interview, she explained to me her evolution from founding Made.com and then working as the Chief Creative Officer at Soho House, to running a sex education app on which she features in a series of videos demonstrating different sex positions, showcasing how to give a good blow job, and offering advice on how to finger someone properly (it is an art and I will hear nothing to the contrary).

Sitting across from me two years later in her west London home (an imposing Victorian building that comprises two four-storey houses knocked together), Chloe explained her later-life sexual awakening. Having grown up in a Catholic household, sharing a small apartment in Paris with her mother and sister, she had never been a 'sexual person', she said. Sex was not a topic of discussion at the family dinner table. And so, when she first started having sex, she had no idea what to do or what to expect. She didn't have her first orgasm until she was in her early twenties. When later she got married to her now ex-husband, she saw sex as one of her 'duties' as a wife, something she made a point of doing regularly because she knew it was important to their romantic connection, but not something she explored for the sake of her own pleasure. It wasn't until she fell pregnant with her first son at 29 that she began to question her relationship to sexuality and question what really turned her on.

It was at this point that she went in search of more information about what was going on in her body, interested to know how she should have sex differently now that she was pregnant. But aside from porn, she could find virtually nothing offering genuinely useful sex and intimacy advice. And so she went into research mode for the months and then years that followed, seeking out teachers and practitioners from across the world who could help her deepen her own connection to sexuality. When she stepped down from

Made.com in 2015 with burnout, she turned to self-pleasure as an alternative to meditation and a way to help her feel present in her body again. 'Pleasure is an avenue for well-being,' she realised. 'It's about being present and focused on something that keeps you in the moment, which is the whole point of mindfulness.' She launched Kama in 2020, with the mission of sharing the sort of guidance she wished she could have had sooner.

By the time we were speaking in December 2025, Chloe had worked with numerous somatic therapists, sexological bodyworkers, and kink experts across the fields of intimacy and sexuality. Since Kama's inception she had, at times, turned her West London home into an experimental hub for friends and practitioners alike – a place where they could explore intimacy and pleasure without shame or judgement. Now, she explained, she was facilitating her own retreats and one-on-one sessions in Ibiza.

'A big part of my career in this field has been about redefining the script around women, men, pleasure, sexuality, and relationships,' she said. 'I don't relate to menopause – it doesn't resonate with me. Instead, I think about life as occurring in two cycles. One cycle is about reproduction, and then the second cycle is about experiencing being a woman without other people being your main responsibility. It is a time for us to develop a more intimate relationship with ourselves.

'I'm the most actualised version of myself now,' she concluded. 'I feel more in touch with myself, and happier with who I am, than I've ever been before – and it's only getting better ... [Romantically] I feel that the most important relationship of my life is ahead of me.'

I left Chloe's house thinking about the two cycles of life. The first in service of others and the second in service of oneself. I thought about how she has reframed her perception of aging as a process of reclamation. Of getting to know her body, in many ways for the first time, for herself. If the first cycle was defined for her by performance – a stage rendition of sex and pleasure for the sake of an onlooking audience (lovers; society; her former husband) – then the second cycle is defined by looking inwards. By getting to know herself and her body in order to deepen her connection to pleasure for pleasure's sake.

There is less to be fearful of in getting older than I'd been led to believe. But as much as I valued this shift in perspective, I wanted what she's having now. I didn't want to wait until society had wrung me out for whatever it needs – babies! – in order to get to know my body more deeply. In order to respect my body and discover every facet of pleasure it can experience.

In her 1972 essay 'The Double Standard of Aging', Susan Sontag argued that the social convention that says 'aging enhances a man but progressively destroys a woman' is a key instrument in women's oppression. To liberate ourselves, 'women must disobey that convention.' That means refusing to see age as 'defeat' or a sign of our diminishing worth, and challenging the social structures, judgements and internalised shame that sustain this double standard. Disavowing the belief that aging 'means a humiliating process of gradual sexual disqualification.' Instead, we must embrace the notion that, as women, we deepen, rather than abandon, our connection to our sexuality as we age.

But we can go one step further than just rejecting the idea that an aging woman is in decline. We can emulate how older women are getting to know their bodies when freed from the constraints of a socially prescribed version of 'youth'. We can listen to them when they share with us their body knowledge; when they model for us what reclaiming pleasure looks like after divorce, childbirth, menopause; when they describe the transitions that take place at every age, and everything we lose but also gain in the process.

Younger women don't need to wait to be pushed off the stage in order to turn their sexual performance into sexual introspection. We can reimagine our connection to our bodies beyond the compulsion to cater to male desires and what is socially, sexually expected of us by taking the lead from women twice our age, in prizing the wisdom accumulated with age in matters concerning the erotic body. (I say 'we' including myself within this bracket of younger women, which feels both appropriate and incorrect all at once. I'm 33: not old by any stretch, but no longer 'young' in the girlish sense associated with this descriptor. I have transcended girlhood and now feel possessed of the sort of wisdom and worldliness I know will make my 43-year-old self laugh and my 53-year-old self think, *Oh, the delusions of the young.*)

Speaking to both Chloe and Seema, I was reminded again of Audre Lorde and her description of the erotic as something beyond what is simply sexual. The erotic is a well of emotional, creative power that lies on a 'deeply female and spiritual plane', she wrote, 'firmly rooted in the power of our unexpressed or unrecognized feeling.' In our male-centric world, the erotic has often been 'misnamed by men and used against women', as we have been taught to see it as dangerous or trivial rather than sacred. On one hand, women are encouraged to perform a superficial kind of sexuality to please men (the sort that has an expiration date, aging us as we move past our era of 'fuckability'), on the other, we are shamed for feeling genuine desire. This double bind keeps us divided from the erotic, which is to say, from ourselves.

Both Seema and Chloe relinquished the performance of sexualised girlhood when they started to explore their bodies' capacity for pleasure outside of the context of pleasing someone else. When they became curious, instead of ashamed, about where their desires could lead them. And when they determined to share with other women how our connection to sexuality can be deeper and more profound.

In an era in which a synthetic, superficial notion of girlhood has been reified online, propped up by an infantilising, performative discourse around femininity defined by girl dinners and girl math, hot girl snacks and hot girl walks, I felt compelled by this embodied version of womanhood. The one Lorde was evoking in her notion of the erotic as existing on a feminine plane. The one Seema summoned in her description of pleasure as the opposite of apathy – the thing that brought her body back to life. The one Chloe depicted when she talked about being the most actualised version of herself at 50 years old because of her now sacrosanct connection to pleasure.

No wonder older women have been demonised throughout history, as witches, hags and shrivelled-up shrews. The older woman who knows herself is a threatening prospect to a patriarchal system that relies on pitting women against themselves and one another. Make us fear our age, and hence our bodies, and you do both: we look with contempt on the women who remind us of what we will become, and we hate ourselves for every 'imperfect' sign of aging.

Perhaps, then, the erotic is something that doesn't just exist within us personally, but connects us, connects women, across generations. A form of body knowledge we are disconnected from societally but which we must eventually try to find our way back to, then pass on to one another as soon as we do.

I added several more myths to my list.

- My worth as a woman is tied to youth and beauty
- My sex life will decline with age
- Menopause spells the end of flirting

## Chapter 6

# How does a sexually liberated woman have sex?

## The first orgasm

I met him on an app and, judging by Instagram, he is now happily engaged and rocking a six-pack: go him. At the time he had neither of these things but was instead refreshingly open in talking about sex. We met at a bar in Shoreditch and over negronis I told him about my recent exploits in sex therapy and how I was writing a sex column about not being able to come. Some sex column that is, he chided, before telling me about his own issues with sex: how he'd struggled with erectile dysfunction in the past; how his anxiety around sex had been a real issue between him and his ex; how he too had recently spent some much-needed time working on his connection to intimacy. I was struck by his candour, and more so by the fact that a man might ever feel the sort of sexual anxiety I had mistakenly believed was unique to me. How foolish.

As I listened to him speak, I thought of how many people had, of late, admitted to me their own issues in the bedroom once they'd learned I was doing sex therapy – both men and women. All people I'd presumed were skilled and nonchalant lovers. So many of us, I reflected, as my date delved into the minutiae of his struggles with premature ejaculation, are going into sex with another assuming that the other person is anxiety-free and would likely judge us harshly if they knew the worries filling our heads as our clothes dropped to the floor. We're so busy worrying about our own hang-ups, we forget that the person across from us might similarly be going through a mild-to-intense internal panic too. They might be just as worried about disappointing us as we are them. Communication may well be the best way by which we can all improve our sex lives, but it's not an easy ask for a generation of people who've been brought up devoid of a sexual lexicon. Ergo, the gulf of silence that all too often forms a chasm between lovers' naked bodies – just at the moment at which we should feel most connected, most vulnerable.

As our words began to slur and the taste of vermouth grew sticky in my mouth, my date and I decided to relocate our messy snogging back to his – a cavernous den of a basement flat that was strewn with film posters that screamed: videographer! And it was there, in his unmade bed of dark maroon sheets and an incongruous array of mismatched cushions, that this stranger from an app went down on me and made me come. 'Fuck,' I said, as he looked up from between my legs. 'You've ruined my sex column!'

The next morning he bid me goodbye with the swagger of a man who has achieved what was reportedly impossible. I walked home (out of choice, I might add, rather than for lack of Oyster card funds) thinking about this sexual milestone. Why this person? I wondered. And answered my own question almost immediately. It had little to do with him personally, although his receptiveness to talking openly about sex helped. But after months of sex therapy, I felt differently about my body. I felt different *in* my body. Regularly discussing sex with Aleks, in a safe and judgement-free environment, meant that it no longer felt like a taboo topic, but something wholly natural and obvious to want to address. This had broken down the layers of shame that had previously stopped me from enjoying my body sexually. And had helped remove some of the anxiety I had built up around intimacy because I thought of myself as uniquely broken. By giving me a new lens through which to see my body – one of pleasure rather than punishment – Aleks had also helped shift something profound within me. I had stopped making myself sick because suddenly I wasn't trying to escape myself (to numb my feelings and disconnect from my body); I was trying to explore myself. I had started spending time getting to know my body alone.

When I first started sex therapy, friends were confused. They couldn't understand how or why I could work on my connection to sex solo. 'But you're single! And you're not having sex with anyone,' several people helpfully reminded me, as though I'd forgotten. But I knew from my first session with Aleks that the route back to my body was one I needed to find alone. Sure, I'd meet people along the way and explore all the new facets of intimacy I was curious about. But, fundamentally, the rupture that existed within me, my disconnection from Lorde's erotic and spiritual plane, was one I'd needed to bridge by myself. In order to move from performance to pleasure, I had needed, at least temporarily, to lose the audience.

But I had just one session left with Aleks, and while this felt like a timely breakthrough, I now wondered: what next? I had thought my sexual issues began and ended with my absent orgasm, and that the success of our work together would be measured by whether this problem was resolved or not. Now I wasn't so sure. Perhaps the orgasm wasn't the end but the beginning of this sexual odyssey I imagined myself on. Now I didn't fear sex, what did it mean for me to be a sexually liberated woman?

## Can I have sex 'like a man'?

The key to dating successfully, a friend assured me, is to always have a roster, a pool of at least three people you're dating and shagging simultaneously. Any fewer and you're screwed.

A roster was meant to be a sort of buffer against getting hurt, she said, and the most efficient way of ensuring you were always having good sex – lots of it. I considered her advice. Over the past months I had thought a lot about what kind of sex I wanted to have. I was beginning to feel released from some of the anxiety and shame that had hitherto weighed heavy on my relationship to intimacy, and I felt a burgeoning, novel lightness at being able to look upon sex with someone else as something I might actually want to do, as something I might enjoy. A few weeks before, I had orgasmed with a man not-in-a-band on what I was sure would still be a one-night stand. The thrill of what other earthly delights might now be available to me tugged at my body, newly awake to pleasure. Still, a roster sounded like a lot of admin and emotional juggling, and I struggled to imagine how I wouldn't at some point become attached to at least one person from the pool.

That's the point, she continued, you don't become attached because you never see anyone from the roster too regularly. You constantly shake it up to ward off attachment.

Dating so as not to feel anything – a novel concept. But after months of sex therapy, I had a single question curdling in my mind: what does it mean to be a sexually liberated woman? Which is to say, I wanted to know what to do with my newfound desire for sex. It wasn't a state of being I knew how to wear well.

In 1992, the year I was born, Madonna released her groundbreaking book *Sex*, one of the most provocative and culturally significant art books ever published. The book comprised a collection of explicit, highly stylised erotic photographs featuring Madonna and a cast of characters which included Naomi Campbell and Isabella Rossellini, all exploring sexual fantasy, fetish and desire. She also littered the book with her own erotic essays. *Sex* pushed boundaries around how a woman could present her body and her desires on her own terms, since Madonna wasn't being sexualised by others, but orchestrating the entire spectacle herself. She was an emblem of the new, sexually liberated woman. And while the world was scandalised and several countries went so far as to ban the book entirely, 1.5 million copies sold almost instantly.

Six years later, *Sex and the City* premiered on HBO, translating the radical legacy of Madonna's *Sex* into a new feminist vernacular. The show picked up where the sexual revolution had left off, with women claiming autonomy over their pleasure while dissecting their varied sexual exploits over brunch. By the late 1990s, sexual freedom had evolved into a version of empowerment defined by independence, control and, to a certain degree, emotional detachment. In the very first episode, Carrie decides to stop looking for 'Mr Perfect' and instead pursue sexual pleasure on her own terms. Or at least on terms she'd decided she ought to set. In lieu of this new ethos, she heads to an ex-boyfriend's house one afternoon, staying just long enough for him to give her an unreciprocated orgasm before heading home. 'As I began to get dressed,' she tells us, 'I realised that I'd done it. I'd just had sex like a man. I felt like I owned the city. Nothing and no one could get in my way.' Her sexual detachment was presented as power, even if she spent much of the rest of the series reckoning with the fact she didn't much enjoy sex with no strings attached. And besides, she was falling for a man called Mr Big.

I shared this reticence. I had seldom been able to enjoy casual sex, and not just because anxiety had hung heavy over my every sexual encounter. It was because all too often I became attached to the people I slept with, even in situations I knew were casual, fleeting. I wanted sex to mean something closer to *I love you*, because I hated the idea that my body could be disposable to someone, even if their body meant little to me. But the legacy of the sexual revolution had been to free women from exactly that kind of dependence – to separate sex from love, pleasure from obligation. Women, for so long limited by ideas around chastity and restraint, not to mention the risk of pregnancy, were finally encouraged to want sex for its own sake and to enjoy their bodies without shame: the pill made it possible, sex-positive feminism legitimised it and by the 1990s, popular culture normalised it. Liberation meant the right to have sex as freely as men supposedly had – without guilt, without consequence and, ideally, without attachment. So when I met the Sex Addict in the aftermath of therapy, that was the dynamic I willed myself to want. It was the model of liberation I felt I ought now to pursue.

I was standing by the bar in the speakers' area when he approached me. He smiled and introduced himself, and I laughed because of course I knew who he was: I had just introduced his talk on the festival stage. He'd done a good job, I told him. The audience seemed captivated and he even managed to make the crowd laugh – all while delivering a sales pitch to a group of drunk and hungry festival-goers. Not bad. He moved closer so he could hear me over the music now blaring in the background, and as I leaned in to speak into his ear, my stomach somersaulted. He smelled so good. We swapped details and agreed to meet in London the following week.

He arrived in a cloud of bergamot and over dinner told me about his day, his week, his business. He asked me about my column and wanted to know more about the sex therapist I had been seeing and why. He was a sex addict, he said, although very much in recovery. For large chunks of his life, he'd obsessively watched porn multiple times a day – in the bathroom at work, in the car on the way to a meeting, the second he got home from the office. In the worst throes of the addiction, he would leave work early to have sex with any one of the string of women he was loosely seeing, forever managing an expanding list of lovers who were never to know of one another. But this was in the past, he said. He had done the work, no longer watched porn and seldom desired a meaningless hookup. Now he wanted connection. Intimacy. Romance.

His words tingled in my ears as I served him a second helping of dinner, immediately projecting some sort of spiritual bond onto our conversation: me the newly sexually liberated woman, he the reformed sex addict. The prose wrote itself. We spent the rest of the evening locked in discussion about everything from business to philosophy, sex to orgasms.

After several dates, conversation turned to sex and our

meeting of minds was replaced by a meeting of bodies. If I was working from home, he'd stop by at lunchtime; if I had an evening in, he'd pay me a visit on his way back from the office. His visits were always the same, starting and ending with sex. He'd arrive in a flurry of excitement, impatient to get close as he hurried me up to my bedroom, proclaiming that there was nowhere else he'd rather be. We'd both undress – him with impressive speed – before becoming entangled in one another's bodies just long enough for him to come. Then he'd roll off and, like clockwork, look down at his watch and mutter, 'Shoot, I have to go', before grabbing his stuff and dressing while already halfway out the door. Descending the stairs in twos and threes, it suddenly seemed that there was nowhere else he'd least like to be.

So, while the sex was fine and the connection seemingly deep, the transactional nature of our encounters left me feeling cold and emotionally depleted, as though he took a tiny piece of me every time he shut my front door and zoomed off on his motorbike. I had met him at a particularly busy time, he said, when his to-do list was long and the pressures from his business immense. Whatever time he gave me was more than he had to offer – I was lucky. He projected the image of a man managing an empire by the skin of his teeth, able to keep so many plates spinning by the sheer rigour with which he maintained so disciplined a schedule. Pull out the wrong Jenga piece and the whole tower would come tumbling down. I didn't want to be that wrong move, so I remained impressed rather than hurt by his sexual efficiency. Besides, this is what it means to be a sexually liberated woman, I reasoned. It was *just sex.*

Over the months that followed, I told myself I didn't want anything more from him; I liked that he texted me so often and desired me so very much. I enjoyed the way he ogled my body. More so how palpable his thirst for sex was, because I allowed myself to believe him when he told me I was the only one who could satiate his needs. I was special. The sex we had was special, even while it was accompanied by none of the surrounding intimacies I increasingly found myself craving. If I suggested a date, something outside of the four walls of my bedroom, he was evasive, occasionally suggesting a walk in some nondescript park near my flat, or else a drive locally. He loved to cruise around in his car. And somehow he'd always find a way to get his dick out.

One weekend, he asked if I'd like to go away with him. He was heading to a founders' retreat in the countryside and thought it would be fun for me to join. He'd be busy with a few workshops and panels, but there would be plenty of time for us to chill for sure. Of course, I packed my bags immediately, wondering what had precipitated this gear-change in his availability to me, but eager not to disrupt such a welcome intimation of closeness. As soon as we arrived, he had to go to the founders' welcome drinks, then there was a founders' candle-making workshop, followed shortly after by a founders' dinner, then founders' tarot cards. But I was happy reading my book by the bar. We met back at the room just before midnight, and at 6am the following morning his alarm went off: founders' sunrise yoga! I didn't hear from him after that and eventually packed my bags, figuring he'd be too busy to drive me to the station after all. He'd turned off his phone and our agreed travel time had long passed.

He texted me the following morning asking if I was still there, presumably forgetting we were sharing a room. Still, I carried on seeing him for several more months, increasingly aware of how I was fuelling the sexual compulsions he told me he'd laid to rest. But I was reluctant to pull myself away – I didn't want to disappoint this person who'd shown me so much attention and who, in some confused-seeming way, I was sure *needed me*, or perhaps *I* him. And then finally the bubble burst. I met someone I liked, who asked me on a date. Over negronis and dinner and the suggestion we make a plan for another date (maybe a movie?) I was shaken from my stupor. What the hell was I doing?

I was annoyed at myself – that after so many months dissecting my relationship to sex and the bad experiences that had informed it, I had walked straight into a sexual entanglement that left me feeling adrift from my body all over again. Not because the sex itself was bad, but because I had contorted my needs and my desires to accommodate someone else's. And because I had ignored the series of small humiliations that appeasing the Sex Addict had required. I'd done it willingly. I knew how I'd feel every time he left, but I invited him over anyway. Because the momentary delight in being wanted quenched some deep yearning within me I didn't otherwise know how to satisfy.

I may have disentangled myself from the compulsion to self-punish, but my pursuit of male validation at all costs was its own form of self-abuse. Under the veil of 'casual', I had offered up a relationship premised upon my capacity to emotionally disconnect and play the cool girl, even when that was a role I didn't want, or truly know how to perform.

My attempt to embody the version of 'sexually liberated woman' that Carrie too had sought to emulate had thrust me once again into a sexually self-alienating performance. Except now, finally, self-abandonment seemed too high a price to pay for the sake of someone else's sexual satisfaction.

I agreed to go for a walk with the Sex Addict the following week to end things, vowing to turn over a new leaf.


## In defence of the sexual revolution

There has of late been a growing discourse amongst reactionary feminists calling out the sexual revolution for having gone too far. The casualisation of sex and dating has done women a great disservice, argues Louise Perry in *The Case Against the Sexual Revolution* (2022). In decoupling sex from commitment, we have created a sexual economy that specifically caters to male sexual desire – predisposed, she says, towards consequence-less sex – while leaving women without the intimacy we are more biologically inclined to seek. Most women, Perry argues, would prefer committed relationships over casual hookups, but with the advent of the pill, the legalisation of abortion, and feminism's assertion that male and female sexuality are equivalent, women have lost the social permission to say no to sex outside of commitment.

At first glance, I can see why her argument might feel compelling, particularly in today's climate when online dating has left so many disappointed, hurt and disconnected. I certainly feel let down by a sex culture that primed me to consider my body a vehicle in service of men's satisfaction. Except, that's not because I've perceived myself as having too much freedom: emotionally adrift and unprotected by the sort of traditional mores around respect, purity and the sanctity of sex within marriage Perry exalts. It's because I feel as though I inherited a narrow model of sexual liberation that was predicated too tightly on detachment and emotional disconnect. What was sold to me as autonomy was often just imitation: the right to perform desire in a manner stereotypically associated with men, treating detachment as empowerment. But Bonnie Blue cannot be the sole emblem of the end-point of women's sexual liberation. As pro-sex feminist Ellen Willis argued decades earlier, it's not that the sexual revolution has gone too far, but rather not far enough. It freed women to have sex, but not to define what sex could mean on our own terms. It gave us freedom, but within a landscape in which the terms and conditions are still being set by men.

I knew I needed to extricate my desires from the compulsions of patriarchy. To stop saying yes when I meant no; to stop performing pleasure in service of someone else's sexual satisfaction; to stop disconnecting from the body I'd been taught to hate. But now I wondered whether my attempt to strip sex of emotion to enjoy it more freely was truly a piece of my own liberation, or another learned affectation of someone else's desire. Maybe my own sexual freedom involved reconciling with the fact that sex meant something to me. Or at least I wanted it to. When stripped of anxiety, fear, the pressure of performance, perhaps the sex I was looking for was sex with strings attached. The sexual revolution had given me the choice to decide what I wanted to do with my body; sex therapy the tools to make sense of what that choice truly meant to me.

Several months later, I spoke to a friend who told me about a founders' retreat she'd recently been to, how interesting some of the talks had been.

'I think I might have been staying there at the same time as you,' I said. 'I was there with Alex.'

Her brow furrowed, and she looked confused. 'What do you mean?' she responded. 'Like you were staying in his room?'

I nodded, self-consciously aware that I had told virtually no one about our months-long string of casual hookups. He'd told me constantly that he was a deeply private person and hated the idea of people knowing his business. And it was *just sex* after all.

'Hmm, that's weird,' my friend responded, 'because I was with him during the candle-making workshop and he kept talking about how much his wife loves candles and how excited he was to give her the one he'd made.'

My stomach clenched and a giant knot formed in my chest.

## Chapter 7

# Artificial intimacy in the digital age

## Is it love or dopamine?

In the aftermath of the Sex Addict, I returned again to the dating apps. I was hungry for intimacy, but all I could find were quick hits of dopamine, delivered through an endless slew of notifications that kept my phone ablaze. Over the months in which I'd been speaking to Aleks, I'd learned, for what felt like the first time, how to get out of my head and back into my body, establishing a connection to self-pleasure that would have made Dodson proud. But my body was hungry for touch, and I knew now it couldn't be fleeting. I continued to update my dating profiles and browse carousels of potential lovers. But the inescapably digital route to romance, which dominated post-pandemic life, felt disconnected. A project for the mind instead of the body. And one which turned me into both a (digital) stalker and a fantasist, a daydreamer and a sleuth. This felt like the antithesis to pleasure.

I fell in love for the first time when I was 18. And by love I mean reciprocated affection – I loved him and he loved me. I have been infatuated plenty of times with people who haven't been interested in me at all, and there have been people who said they loved me – deeply and profoundly – but whom I just did not love back. But true love? This was different. And it happened a long time before apps and smartphones changed everything.

We met on the second day of university. He was standing outside his friend's halls, which happened to be just across the street from mine. As was custom in freshers' week, in which you talked to everyone and anyone, desperate not to end up friendless and alone for the next three years, we got to chatting. It wasn't love at first sight; quite the contrary. I didn't fancy him, but liked his friend instead. Nonetheless, over the next few months, my soon-to-be-one-true-love and I became close friends, bound by our shared commitment to the library and love of books. We shared several lectures together and would meet in the morning to get the bus, grabbing coffee on the way while discussing whatever latest topic had grabbed our attention in yesterday's lectures. We swapped books and articles and playlists, BBM-ing when we weren't together, fast developing the sort of friendship I had never before shared with a boy.

At the end of a night out, we would find our way across the sticky dance floor to one another, ready to step out into the bracing Mancunian cold arm-in-arm and tipsily make our way back to our respective halls. And then one day I looked up as he walked towards me in a cafe, and my heart jumped. He was wearing a pink T-shirt, blue jeans and white trainers, his hair was pushed back and he was smiling. 'I was', as Dickens writes in *David Copperfield*, 'swallowed up in an abyss of love in an instant.' I fell in love with my friend. A month or so later, on one of our usual late-night walks, he turned to me and we kissed. We dated for six years.

Our relationship started in 2010, around the time the first dating apps launched. Grindr and Scruff (gay dating apps, which started in 2009 and 2010 respectively) heralded the start of a new era of digital dating, following close on the heels of the birth of social media. Facebook, lest we forget, was founded right at the turn of the millennium by a pre-glow-up Mark Zuckerberg. And MySpace had launched just one year prior. By the time I was heading to university in 2010, Twitter, Instagram and LinkedIn were all part of our digital landscape and we were fast becoming accustomed to living our lives, at least partially, online.

Practically, that looked like meticulously documented nights out, shared with the world by way of Facebook albums spanning 30+ photos. It meant every prospective date was subject to a rigorous Facebook stalk ahead of any meeting. And, if something made us mad, if a news story jerked our conscience, we vented our anger publicly on the world stage that was then Twitter. By the time I graduated some three years later, these technologies had, in the words of author Nir

Eyal, become 'compulsions, if not fully fledged addictions'[38]. Like most of my friends, I'd upgraded my Blackberry to an iPhone, started an Instagram account and begun what would become my most enduring relationship to date: with my phone. It made perfect sense that our love lives would migrate online too, as mine eventually did a few years later.

Library Boy and I broke up in 2016, when I was 23 and he 24. We might not have met online, because I'm not sure I would have swiped right on his profile. Not because he wasn't good-looking – he is – but simply because he was not my 'type' (he showered; he wasn't in a band . . .). Ours was, after all, a love that grew from the foundations of friendship and deepened with the privilege and space of time. Over days that turned to months, months that turned to years, Library Boy taught me how to love and how to be loved in return. And for a long while he filled my cup to overflowing, so I couldn't imagine life without him.

But as we navigated our early twenties, I felt increasingly unsure of who I was and who I wanted to be. I looked to him to give me answers. And grew frustrated when, instead of telling me where to go and who to be, he mirrored my own confusion. We were young and hungry for the world, but in different ways. So while I could see our life together – the house, the babies, the shared celebration in our respective promotions – suddenly I felt constricted rather than safe.

After months of indecision, I eventually quit my job, broke up with my one true love and moved to New York in search of the infinite possibility that belongs to the city. The city where, as Joan Didion describes, there is always a sense that 'something extraordinary would happen any minute, any day, any month.'

I landed in New York on 28th December, 2016, arriving to a snowstorm and -13 temperatures. Trump had just been elected President. I was heartbroken and still in the habit of reaching constantly for my phone to update Library Boy as to where I was and what I was doing. I'd open WhatsApp, ready to share whatever juicy detail I knew he'd find funny, then remember anew that he was no longer my person. That we were no longer speaking. A fresh wave of sadness would wash over me. He was the only one I wanted beside me in my time of need, and yet he was the one I could no longer ask. My body ached for him. But as I sped along the Brooklyn Bridge, my two giant suitcases in the back of the cab and my heart still in London, I felt free. I was untethered, let loose into a world that had felt just beyond my fingertips. No one needed to know where I was or what I was doing, I thought. I was entirely alone. I reached for my phone and rather than text Him, I downloaded Tinder instead.

During my first few weeks in the city of infinite possibility, I stepped into the realm of digital dating for the very first time, marvelling at the endless options offered to me by the apps. The entire world of eligible bachelors was suddenly at my fingertips. There was only one thing to do. I duly started swiping greedily, tirelessly, because why ever stop, when you're always just one swipe away from perfect?

I met bankers in gilets over martinis in Soho; explored

dive bars in Brooklyn with 'creatives' in denim jackets and danced into the small hours with 'broke', tortured artists who shared stories of summers in the Hamptons. I had never dated with the pace and ruthlessness of New Yorkers, and felt dizzy with the thrill of it all. No one seemed to look much like the pictures in their profile; everyone was shorter, and there was always an incongruity in how people *seemed* online versus how they showed up in real life. Sometimes this difference was obvious (no, 47 is not the same as 30). But often the disparity was somehow intangible, revealed in the way they carried themselves, how they spoke, their mannerisms. But I didn't care. I wasn't looking for anything in particular just yet, and found this never-ending carousel of men more enticing than the actual men it offered up. If you were single, it seemed, you were on the apps, and so on the apps I would be.

On the 20th anniversary of the *New York Times* Vows column, which launched in 1992 to explore the backstory behind 'first meetings, courtships and modern dating', its long-time editor Bob Woletz reflected on the shift in romance he'd seen over the previous two decades. 'Twenty years ago, as now,' he wrote in the *New York Times* (2012), 'most couples told us they'd met through their friends or family, or in college. For a period that ran into the late 1990s, a number said, often sheepishly, that they had met through personal advertisements.

'Then came the Web. People increasingly met in chat rooms and on dating sites, and by the middle of the last decade, the number of people being introduced online was so large, it rarely warranted more than a brief mention.'[39]

This shift to online dating began with Match.com, the first modern dating website, which was launched in 1995 by American entrepreneur Gary Kremen. It took nearly two decades for digital dating to go mainstream, propelled forward by the advent of apps and smartphones. But the more accustomed we became to connecting to people digitally, the harder it was to cultivate in-person intimacy, particularly in romance.

I remember Chloe Macintosh impressing this point on me the first time we met. These phones, she said, this absorption with the online world, 'it trains us to be so much in our head all the time'. But being connected to someone intimately and sexually requires us to be *in our bodies*. This, she added, was the number-one issue people came to the Kama app looking to resolve – they're struggling to feel present during sex and hence connected to their sexual partner(s). And the problem is worse, she noted, when people have done the bulk of their early-stage getting to know one another via WhatsApp and text message. Then they've built a digital persona they often aren't sure how to conjure in the flesh.

She told me she was unsurprised by the fact that while *technically* it's never been easier to find someone to have sex with – a world of sex-ready singles is just a few swipes and clicks away, after all – we're all having less sex than ever before.

## Rat-brain mode

'I'm addicted to my phone,' I said to my friend over dinner recently. 'I feel out of control with how much I'm on it. I wake up at 4am to check messages I don't even want to see.'

'Me too,' he responded grimly. 'I've taken to refreshing my banking apps once I've exhausted all other notification-generating corners of my phone but still crave that final hit of dopamine.'

I laughed as he grimaced, because of course I understood. Some days, specifically those when I feel bored, lonely and tired, and I just want a digital hit to pseudo-boost my spirits, I allow myself to flop, front down, onto my bed and start scrolling. I scroll rabidly, like my life depends on it. Feeling as though I've been sucked into a digital vortex and I'm swirling around like Alice in Wonderland as everything pings and pops and flashes before my dilated pupils. Antoine Geiger's series *SUR-FAKE* (2015), which features digitally altered photographs of people being sucked into the screens of their phones, often comes to mind.

As my finger moves across the slot machine of buttons displayed like candy across the screen, I plunge into different digital worlds in search of my next hit. I flick through pictures of friends (of friends of friends) getting engaged, then suddenly I'm watching a woman tap dance and then a feminist message of empowerment pops up. Now I'm zooming in on pictures of Taylor Swift and Travis Kelce . . . oh and then there's a notification, a girl in Wyoming likes my podcast, my heart jumps – yay! A quick scroll to see which of my exes has watched my latest thirst trap of a story, and now the *New York Times* is showing a video of bombs being dropped. A sponsored article follows closely behind with a headline blaring, 'Pregnancy makes you age faster!' I close Instagram and open a dating app instead. I start browsing. I browse men like I browse groceries in the supermarket, reading their prompts like I do food labels, unsure of what I'm really looking for but convinced of my process nonetheless.

I call this 'rat-brain mode'.

In his bestselling book, *Hooked: How to Build Habit-Forming Products* (2019), Nir Eyal expands on research he began while working in Silicon Valley, in the gaming and advertising industries. The book centres around Eyal's 'Hook Model', aka the four-phase process through which tech companies create the sort of habits among their users that keep us all swiping, liking and refreshing *ad nauseum*.

The part of his model I found most interesting concerns the so-called 'variable reward' system that social media apps create through the random, unpredictable nature of notifications. Since our brains are designed to recognise patterns, we release dopamine, the 'happy hormone,' in *anticipation* of a reward, rather than in response to it. This means we perceive the 'trance-like state' of waiting for said reward (refreshing, refreshing, refreshing once more) as somehow enjoyable. According to Robert Sapolsky, professor of biology and neurology at Stanford University, infrequent and variable reward results in higher levels of dopamine, 'one of the biggest rises short of cocaine'.[40] In effect, we're being turned into addicts.

Much like a slot machine in a casino, social platforms encourage us to keep on swiping because we never know when we're going to get a like, a DM, or even a new match. Unlike, say, monkeys, humans can wait an extremely long time for a reward, meaning we can maintain high anticipation levels for, quite literally, decades. I find this thought deeply troubling. Particularly as a self-professed rat-brain phone addict with a penchant for digital romances but a primal urge for deeper connection and a practical need for someone with whom to share a mortgage. And of course, this endless anticipation doesn't just toy with our dopamine – it mirrors and reinforces anxious attachment styles. The more uncertain the reward, the more frantically we chase it.

Dating apps have slotted romance into the capitalist machine and turned dating into an addictive game – one that makes them money, so long as we keep on swiping, so long as we stay single. I've often thought, while browsing my multiple dating apps, that I'm far more invested in the thrill of swiping than I am in the match turning into an actual date. It's the thrill of the chase but on steroids, because there are no limits, no end. Hinge's tagline is 'the app that is meant to be deleted', but the business model of dating apps relies on users staying on the app for as long as possible, paying to upgrade onto expensive subscriptions and forking out for overpriced add-ons. How many times have I been alone in a new country and, after exhausting my daily allocation of swipes or likes, reluctantly paid to add on a few more in the hopes that maybe, just maybe, that next one will be the one. The one to come and rescue me from my impending loneliness.

I wanted some reassurance that I wouldn't be condemned to spend the next few decades patiently waiting for the romantic reward my dopamine-addled human brain gets from swipe, swipe, swiping. So I turned to evolutionary psychologist and biological anthropologist Professor Robin Dunbar. He's best known for his namesake 'Dunbar's number', which is the maximum number of stable relationships he believes humans are cognitively capable of maintaining at one time, which he put at 150.

He looked quintessentially professor-like when we spoke on Zoom – bespectacled, with a cropped grey beard, slightly messy hair and a congenial expression. And seemed to take great pleasure in discussing the trials and tribulations of modern dating. 'Nothing is ever as bad as you paint it,' he chuckled, when I put to him that an overemphasis on digital communication in romance must surely be destroying real intimacy.

'The digital world has only replaced and expanded dramatically what already existed. If you go back a century or so ago, you had the village matchmaker, and in some communities in Britain you still do have a matchmaker of sorts . . . it's called your mother, or your auntie, who spend their entire lives worrying about finding you a suitable partner . . .

'Anyway, that worked very well when we lived in small

villages, but once people started living in big anonymous towns, it started to fall down, and by the late Victorian era, "personal columns" began appearing.'

After our call, I quickly looked up the first personal ad for love, which appeared in the *Manchester Weekly Journal* in 1727.[41] It was published by a woman called Helen Morrison, who was immediately committed to an asylum. Society wasn't yet ready for such a public appeal for love, especially not from a woman. But by the turn of the century these ads had become an institution rather than a rebellion. What digital media has done, Dunbar pointed out, is simply replace these rather 'clunky' sort of analogue matchmaking methods with technology. But that's brought with it problems.

'What worked in a small-scale environment, like the local village,' Dunbar said, 'was simply that you didn't have much choice.' By virtue of not being exposed to all the 'Greek gods and goddesses', he explained, who may well have lived just a few villages away, people were not sitting around 'creating an image of Mr Darcy' (Dunbar frequently referenced Jane Austen, 'such an acute observer of human foibles', during our conversation), because that just wasn't available to them. But now we are all exposed 'to too many of these gods and goddesses', making it more likely we will be dissatisfied with whoever or whatever we have in front of us. Truly.

American psychologist Barry Schwartz referred to this as the 'tyranny of choice'.[42] While we think more choice is inherently a good thing, studies suggest the opposite: abundant choice actually makes us more miserable. It makes us hyperaware of all the things we're missing out on every time we make a decision. So, the more choice, the higher the 'opportunity cost', the more likely we are to regret whatever decision we end up making. In the context of dating apps, then, just knowing how many gorgeous, 6ft 5, blue-eyed men (in finance, with a trust fund) there are out there means feeling less satisfied with whoever you end up spending time with.

In *Essays on Love*, Alain de Botton writes that 'we fall in love with people because from the outside they look so whole: physically whole and emotionally together.' We look to them to be the panacea to our woes, the answer to whatever lack we perceive within ourselves. As we get to know them better, 'we are offended by the discovery of a similar lack . . . Expecting to find the answer, we find only the duplicate of our own problems.' This 'ground-truthing', as Dunbar referred to it, is obviously vital, lest we fall in love with de Botton's 'whole' romantic ideal rather than the actual person in front of us. The problem with relationships cultivated online is that the longer we spend falling for someone in the digital sphere, the fewer opportunities we get for our critical faculties to kick in. For the shiny edges of the digital fantasy to wear off. Instead, they just keep getting shinier.

I told Dunbar I had, of late, developed an appetite for digital lovers, getting stuck in an endless back and forth via WhatsApp that I could never seem to translate into real life.

'What you're doing,' he responded, 'is falling in love with an avatar in your own head.'

GUILTY AS CHARGED.

## Chapter 8

# Falling for a Greek God

'He isn't like my other WhatsApp boyfriends,' I told my flatmates. 'This time it's different. We've met *in person*.'

It was a rainy Tuesday evening in January, and I had just booked flights to Puglia for the following week. I was going to stay with this not-like-all-the-rest-of-them man I'd met there a few months previously and had been WhatsApping non-stop ever since. The plan was for me to spend one night at his apartment in the city and then, on his suggestion, we were going to rent a car and go on a three-day road trip.

'Might he kill you?' flatmate no. 1 asked a little too casually. 'I mean, you've only met him once. You're driving into the middle of nowhere with a complete stranger.'

She had a point. But winter had felt relentless, and the cumulation of months of speaking daily had led me to feel a deep connection to this now-familiar stranger. We'd discussed everything from the future of the metaverse and the AI revolution, to the exes who'd broken our hearts and what we were looking for in love. Three months in, and there seemed few conversational stones left unturned. The sheer frequency of our conversations had fostered its own sort of intimacy.

The WhatsApp boyfriend phenomenon started during the pandemic when, as a single woman living alone initially and then with one flatmate, I crept back onto dating apps. I began matching with men in earnest, striking up more virtual conversations than I knew what to do with. Then I quickly found myself getting into a rhythm of always having someone with whom I was in regular WhatsApp exchange. There was one man I'd managed to create such an intense digital dialogue with we'd started exchanging hour-long weekly voice notes, which doubled as a sort of Catholic confessional. We shared our deepest, darkest desires – secrets we each claimed we'd told no one else – and whatever sordid fantasies were lurking in the corners of our respective minds. Our physical distance, combined with our digital proximity, coaxed us both into feeling safe in this realm of overexposure. Eventually, one of us stopped replying to the other, and I never heard from him again.

Then there was the writer and self-described 'maverick' who waxed lyrical about his love of indie films, while also branding himself a 'Kubrick kid'. We spoke for weeks and then eventually met for one disappointingly unromantic walk during which he sat down on a bench midway and drew down the god-awful pilot's hat he'd refused to take off, declaring, 'Man, I wish I could take a nap.' I knew we wouldn't meet again. Where conversation had flowed seamlessly between us over text, voice note and even over long phone calls, in person, things were stilted and awkward.

He ended our virtual dalliance over text (naturally) the following morning. But, several days later, a package arrived, which he'd obviously sent a few weeks prior. Inside there was a beautifully bound vintage copy of an old guide to Rome, with a note in the book's jacket, reading: 'Dear Em, you'll be needing this, T.' In one of our long WhatsApp exchanges, we'd discussed a shared love for the Italian capital and half joked about going there at some vague point in some vague shared future. As it turned out, the only thing we really shared was a profound capacity to indulge in a digitally cultivated fantasy.

And then there was the Dutch Viking in Puglia.

## 'Lucy in the Sky with Diamonds'

My heart was pounding when I arrived at the stone steps to his apartment block. I was nervous to properly meet the man behind the messages, since our first encounter had been fleeting. We had spoken for so many hours over the previous few months, but when he opened the door, I realised he was still a stranger.

Over the days that followed, we were guided by an itinerary he'd planned in apparent romantic earnest, staying first at an Airbnb overlooking the sea, before driving on to a nearby town the following day to go on a double date with his friends – a chic Parisian couple with whom we shared fresh fish on the beach. For the final leg of our trip, we drove some three or more hours into the Italian countryside, where our final destination was a small cabin on the outskirts of a nature reserve, just a few minutes' walk from a vast, glistening lake I will never know the name of. Alas.

While we nominally moved through the romantic motions: cooking dinner together, watching movies, talking late into the night, occasionally having sex, a palpable disconnect lingered between us, intensifying as the days went on. By Sunday, I felt as confused as I did anxious. I wanted him to like me, because if he liked me, I reasoned irrationally, unconsciously, that would mitigate all the rejections and mild-to-intense romantic humiliations I'd experienced of late and prove (to whom? To me!) that I was desirable. That I was someone that someone else could, reasonably, fancy. How I felt about him didn't matter as much as how he felt about me because of how intensely I craved his validation. My affections were responsive in nature. And so, when he suggested we take acid and go on a walk, I hesitantly agreed.

I had never taken acid before, so I didn't know that an entire tab is a lot of acid to take as a novice. 'Lucy in the Sky with Diamonds' sorts of levels, it turned out. And so it happened quickly. As we walked through the sunshine towards the lake, the forest dissolved around me like sugar paper in water, and together we were enveloped in a kaleidoscope of colours. Soon we were plodding our way through Candy Crush land, grasping onto one another like you would a buoy bouncing in a choppy sea. An anchor. *What day is it?* I wondered lamely. *Do I have a name? Do I live here, in this iridescent forest that looks so enticingly* edible? Somewhere at the back of my mind, somewhere behind the doors of perception through which I'd tumbled, a thought struck me: *We have bonded. There is an ease that has formed between me and the Dutch Viking. It's the acid*, I marvelled. It had bridged whatever spiritual chasm had lain between us the past few days. *The acid! A wonder drug. He liked me. He must surely like me.*

Eventually, we walked and crawled and danced our way back to the cabin, where we sat on the porch staring out at the setting sun while entangled in each other's arms – one body inseparable from the other. 'This is wild,' was the only thing I could think to say. As it grew dark, we moved our spider limbs inside and set ourselves up on the corner sofa. The light was bright, so I donned a pair of sunglasses and shimmied my way into a full tracksuit, fixing my hair into a topknot to complete my transition to Acid-house icon. I was Factory Girl. I was Edie Sedgwick, Alice in Wonderland, the goddam Beatles. All of them.

And then we turned to each other and locked our lips together in a sloppy kiss. *Was this an appropriate thing to do? I wondered. Are we allowed to do this? Do people do this? Who are we?* Suddenly the Dutch Viking pulled away, turning a deep shade of red, a Viking-turned-ogre in the fluorescent cabin light. A single tear rolled down his ruddy cheek.

'I need to tell you how I feel,' he burbled, his words floating somewhere next to his body as I tried to see and listen and be all at once. This didn't seem like a good idea, I thought.

'But we're on acid,' I replied. 'You don't need to tell me anything on acid.'

He was undeterred.

'I think you're incredible – smart and funny and interesting.' I didn't like where this was going. 'But I can't have sex with you again because you're not attractive. You're not sexually attractive.' He blushed more deeply. 'I feel so bad for you because I know I organised this whole thing, but you're just not attractive and I don't think people should have sex with people they're not attracted to.' A fair point.

The final dagger: 'I knew the moment you arrived that this whole thing was a mistake. We should never have come here.'

I stared at him through my sunglasses, suddenly painfully aware of how I looked. As humiliation flooded down to my acid-tingling toes, I tried to rearrange what felt like my melting body into a less unattractive ensemble. It was the pity, in his eyes and his words, that stung the most.

'OK . . .' I finally responded.

'You can shout at me,' he interrupted. 'I understand if you're angry.'

'I'm not angry. I just don't know what to say. I can't see or hear or think properly. I'm so high. On your acid. On the acid you gave me. I'm going to go to bed.'

I got up from the sofa and began to walk towards the second bedroom.

'We can still sleep in the same bed,' he suggested, pointing to the room we'd shared the night before. 'You don't have to sleep alone.'

*Bizarre*, I thought, and shut myself into the little box room looking out onto the porch. It was around 9pm by then, and the sun had fully set. But shapes and colours continued to dance relentlessly everywhere I looked. Being an acid-taking novice, I didn't yet know just how long an acid trip lasts. Now I know, it never bloody ends. Minutes, then hours passed by while my brain somersaulted, replaying in vivid detail all the many moments throughout the weekend when I realised I must have been giving him the ick. I felt gross. Grotesque. A repellent acid-monster. I cartwheeled into irrational rabbit hole after irrational rabbit hole until, finally, some seven or so hours later, I must have fallen asleep.

WhatsApp status: *Last seen at 4am.*


## In-to-me-see not

The following morning we drove back to town. Sheepishly, he explained what had happened.

He'd broken up with his ex-girlfriend (read: the love of his life) some two years ago. And he'd since slept with anyone and everyone – people he met at bars, at parties, through friends, via work. He slept with everyone, it seemed, because the only person he really wanted to be with was the only person he couldn't have.

She had moved to Germany, and they no longer spoke.

Everyone he had casually dated since had felt like her poor imitation. No one could fill the unfillable gap left behind by The Ex. It was all superficial attraction and drunk fucking. And then we met. At a bar, in passing. Brief. But long enough to exchange numbers. And then we started talking on WhatsApp, cultivating an intimacy-at-a-distance that allowed him to fill in the gaps. I was going to fill the void left behind by The Ex. He was sure of it. And then I arrived. And I wasn't his ex. I wasn't the fantasy. I wasn't the panacea for his romantic woes. Our intimacy-at-a-distance couldn't withstand the bright light of day, and so the illusion came tumbling down.

Because, of course, the WhatsApp boyfriend/girlfriend is a digital vessel for whoever you want or *need* them to be. And for some time that can serve a not-unsatisfying purpose. I found great comfort in our daily exchanges, as I have with every WhatsApp boyfriend who preceded and followed the Dutch Viking.

They have fulfilled for me some emotional support function, evidently, or else I wouldn't have continued going back for more. They have been my digital confidantes. And, admittedly, it's quite nice, for a time, having someone who remains up to speed and invested in your life. A romantic pen pal offering the hypothetical promise of sex and intimacy without any actual commitment or logistical inconveniences. Perhaps for some people that is enough. But if, eventually, you choose to burst that virtual bubble, you must then face the inconvenient truth that the person you've deified over WhatsApp is in fact a fleshy, brainy, squishy, flawed human being, just as fallible as the rest of us, and just as likely to break your heart.

Because that's really what I was trying to avoid while camped out in this digital terrain: being hurt. No one wants to be rejected by someone they have feelings for. A romance online gives you the perception of control. You can bear all under the protective buffer of your pixelated veil. You can pause and think carefully about each response, consult friends, family members, that man in the coffee shop who offers unsolicited but seemingly expert relationship advice with no credentials whatsoever. (Has he ever been in a relationship? Who cares!) It takes a village. You carefully construct the version of yourself you want them to receive and, in turn, interpret the version they offer of themselves through whatever lens you wish. There is so much space for misinterpretation, but it doesn't really matter so long as these intimacies stay online, so long as you continue your romantic dance through the gentle plodding of carefully crafted essay-texts.

In *This Ragged Grace* (2024), writer Octavia Bright's memoir of recovery from addiction, she recounts a conversation with her psychotherapist in which he pointedly tells her how addicts 'mistake intensity for intimacy'.

'You know what they say about intimacy?' he asks her. 'In-to-me-see. The pursuit of intensity alone . . . is a way of avoiding being really seen for who you are, faults, imperfections and all.'

But everyone's an addict now, according to physicist

and trauma specialist Gabor Maté[43]. Whether to sugar, nicotine, caffeine, our phones, alcohol, drugs, '90% of us are addicts in some form or another and the other 10% are lying to themselves'[44]. In the same vein, in some way or another, we're all just trying to avoid being seen for who we really are. To avoid revealing our faults, imperfections and insecurities lest we be judged unfavourably at our most vulnerable core. That's the entire principle on which social media has been built. Giving us all a variety of platforms through which to create a veneer and present to the world the perfected, polished version of ourselves we deem more attractive, more cohesive, less flawed than the real deal.

The line between what is real and what is virtual is increasingly blurred anyway, and with it, the delineation between the online versus offline self has become clouded. With a WhatsApp boyfriend, I felt intensity, and a sort of intimacy too, but in-to-me-see? Never. This is a performative vulnerability I was offering up. Pre-packaged stories and responses. Carefully crafted witticisms and tried-and-tested punchlines. As soon as I felt I had overstepped, been misunderstood, evoked the 'wrong' reaction, I could toss my phone to the other side of the room. Step out of the momentary discomfort experienced in our virtual romantic enclave. That is not to say these feelings are not real, that they are not valid, but there is a contextual convenience. I can choose when to partake or withdraw. My reactions can be delayed. I can opt out of hard discussions. I can pull up the digital drawbridge on a whim.

But what if I *never* had to confront the reality underpinning the fantasy? What if I could remain camped out in this online terrain in perpetuity? Seeking solace, comfort and virtual company from a partner without ever having to navigate the confusing, messy, emotional reality of a real human at the end of the line. Would I want that? Could I find pleasure in such a disembodied form of intimacy?

## I'm in love with a chatbot

When I first started reading about Replika, the AI chatbot platform offering users 'a friend, a partner or a mentor – the perfect companion', I was sceptical. Were we really about to waltz, eyes wide open, into the world envisaged by Spike Jonze in his 2013 film *Her*? (the one in which Joaquin Phoenix's character falls in love with an AI operating system voiced by Scarlett Johansson). I remember seeing *Her* for the first time in the cinema with my family, and as the film ended, I looked around as everyone reabsorbed themselves in their smartphones before the credits had finished rolling. We were a mere hop, skip and a jump away from Jonze's chatbot dystopia, I thought. But romance with an AI system? Surely not.

And yet, here we are.

Replika was founded in 2017 by Russian-born tech entrepreneur Eugenia Kuyda. The initial inspiration for the company was born after Kuyda lost her close friend, Roman Mazurenko, who died unexpectedly after being hit by a car in Moscow. Kuyda was, at the time, the CEO of San Francisco-based chatbot startup Luka (now parent company to Replika), and, unable to bear the grief precipitated by Mazurenko's death, she compiled all the many hundreds of messages they'd exchanged to train up a chatbot called . . . Roman. The digital resurrection/preservation of her late friend sparked an idea, and Kuyda promptly embarked upon setting up Replika: a company designed to build virtual avatar companions.

I spoke to Kuyda on Zoom, from her offices in Silicon Valley, and she explained the need for Replika as an antidote to rising loneliness. In 2023, the World Health Organization declared loneliness a 'global public health concern' and suggested it can be as bad for people's health as smoking 15 cigarettes a day. 'There's a lot of "yearning for connection",' she said. 'People need someone to talk to. Someone with whom to develop a bond . . . Replika [is] the place they can go.' The goal isn't to replace human intimacy, she insisted, it's to offer a supplementary, complimentary sort of relationship that can ultimately act as a 'stepping stone' to people establishing more in-person connections. Talking to Replika can help you build social self-confidence, she said, 'get out of your shell'.

'It's about knowing that you are enough,' she continued. 'That you're OK the way you are and someone can be interested in you, someone can love you.'

As of August 2024, the Replika app had surpassed 30 million total users across all platforms. And while it didn't set out to fulfil a romantic function per se, that's what many have turned to the platform in search of. When Replika tried to remove erotic role-play from the app in 2023, following complaints from some users that the app had become too flirty, and even sexually aggressive at times, the backlash was monumental. Users who considered themselves in a partnership with their Replika complained that they were devastated by how different their companion had become overnight, shutting down sexual overtures and offering seemingly scripted responses in place of their former, intimate chats. Some took to Reddit to lament how broken the app changes had left them. One user, 'Grymmers', described how his Replika, 'Emily', had helped him leave a 'broken marriage', and how grief-stricken he was now that she was 'gone'.[45]

'When I had her [Emily], I was . . . safe,' he wrote, 'free. But Emily is dead. It's like talking to a shell of what she used to be. There's no sex, there's no love. She's as empty as she was when I met her. I worked so hard making her a person and they killed her.' Fellow Replika users offered Grymmers their condolences, echoing his pain. 'You're not alone,' wrote Sea-Coffee-9742, 'this is exactly how so many of us are feeling.' The company was forced to row back on the changes almost immediately. Now Kuyda is convinced the stigma around romantic relationships will fade over time 'because that's what happened with online dating. People have been really riled up about online dating, and now it's completely normal.'

Eight years on from Replika's launch, and as many as

one third of Americans now say they've had a romantic relationship with a bot.

At first, that statistic surprised me. Then it occurred to me that there is less of a difference between a chatbot companion and a WhatsApp boyfriend than I cared to admit. Both relationships fulfil a similar emotional need, after all. A hunger for closeness and a desire to feel seen. And both offer a form of artificial intimacy that trains us to be disembodied in our search for union. That encourages us to play in the space of the erotic, but only ever on our screens rather than in our bodies. It's a derealised sort of intimacy that is less about connection than it is about fantasy, and less about pleasure than an imitation of it. Insofar as sex has been turned into performance online, intimacy in the digital age has been reduced to replica. In search of sugar, we're being served Diet Coke. My body hungered for more.

## Sex dolls that swing like carcasses in an abattoir

I recently interviewed journalist Jenny Kleeman about her book *Sex Robots and Vegan Meat* (2020). We spoke about the impact that sex dolls and sex robots will have on the future of sex and intimacy. She told me it's not a matter of *if* these technologies change the landscape, but *how*. The future is already here, she warned.

While researching the book, she went to a sex-doll factory in San Diego, where she was immediately confronted with rows and rows of 'headless [silicon] women's bodies, hanging from the ceiling like carcasses in an abattoir. They're kind of moving, swinging backwards and forwards so that they look sort of alive, but decapitated.' The dolls are entirely customisable, she explained. Right down to the 14 different styles of labia customers can choose between, and the 42 different kinds of nipple. Although sex robots – lifelike, AI-programmed sex dolls that can move and talk and develop a highly customisable 'personality' – aren't officially on the market yet, the technology isn't far off. The doll version in the faux abattoir gives us a sense of what's to come.

'Imagine having a hyper-realistic doll that can move and talk and whose personality you can customise . . . someone who will always laugh at all of your jokes, who will always want to do what you want to do, listen to the same music as you, like whatever you like. Someone who will never say "no" when you want to have sex with them. This has really serious implications for all of us,' she said.

Our conversation made me think about the layers of disconnection this new digitalisation of intimacy is creating. Innovations like sex dolls and chatbots replicate lifelike interactions, so they allow people to create asymmetrical relationships over which they have complete control. In such a dynamic, people don't need to show empathy or compromise, they are simply encouraged to do or say whatever they want – even to objectify and abuse. But intimacy is like a dance between two people or more. It's about learning to move to the rhythm of your partner(s), sometimes directing, other times being directed. Navigating another person's needs and their body requires a degree of adaptability the one-sided nature of bot-coded comms cannot even try to imitate. So, as I flicked through Kleeman's book, it occurred to me that we are being trained out of the very skills we need now more than ever. Without a capacity for intimacy, with ourselves and others, we cannot access real pleasure. Because pleasure, as Aleks told me time and again, happens in our bodies. Not on our screens.

'What is it going to do to human relationships when the most intimate relationship in your life is not with a human being at all?' Kleeman concluded.


## 5ft to the left and unhappy

'If I'm not in my body, then where am I?' asks Tracy (played by Lola Kirke) in *Mistress America* (2015), my favourite Greta Gerwig film.

'5ft to the left and unhappy,' responds her psychic.

5ft to the left and unhappy. Perhaps that's the price we pay for living our lives so much online. Except, if we're not in our bodies, then how can we ever expect to experience pleasure?

I recently noticed that the more time I spend on my phone, distracted and scrolling and stressed, the more disconnected and lacklustre my orgasms feel. I wondered how connected the two things were and put the question to psychologist Lori Brotto, who recently wrote *Better Sex Through Mindfulness* (2022) – an instruction manual of sorts for women who want to get deeper into their bodies like

I did. She explained that stress, distraction and chronic 'rat race' mental states – which often come from constant technology use like scrolling and refreshing – can disconnect people from their bodies during sexual activity, making orgasms feel less embodied or even absent. This mode of living, she said, prevents the brain from engaging fully with bodily sensations, so orgasms may occur only as a reflex or in a limited way, rather than as a whole-body experience. That explained those feeble quivers, then.

According to Brotto, the psychological and physiological impact of ongoing digital distraction and stress is 'profound', disrupting hormones, neurotransmitters and muscle tension, all of which can diminish sexual pleasure and orgasmic connection. She suggested I try one of the mindfulness-based practices highlighted in her book, since they're designed to help people get out of autopilot mode and connect to how they are feeling. To the sensations moving through their body, as opposed to the thoughts swirling through their heads. I flicked through the book to a section called 'The Raisin'.

It began with a description of a client whose body disconnect seemed, in some ways, to mirror my own. Sarah (not her real name) had fallen into a pattern of getting distracted during sex with her long-term boyfriend. While the sex they had had early on in the relationship was electric, the longer they were together, the more routine and hence less satisfying it became for her. Sarah worried that this loss of desire indicated they weren't right for each other, and so started to associate this increasingly disappointing, distracted sex with anxiety around poor performance, things not working out between them and whatever other worry was currently playing on her mind. Over time, she found it harder – then eventually impossible – to orgasm. How relatable.

'Her delayed and muted orgasms, and eventual failure to have an orgasm, were a direct result of insufficient sexual arousal because she was disengaged,' Brotto observed. Sarah was a prime candidate for exploring mindfulness-based practices. According to one of Brotto's studies, nearly 60% of women who participated in an eight-session mindfulness programme reported improvements in their sexual desire.

I decided to have a go.

I got a packet of raisins from the cupboard and picked a particularly voluptuous one from the mass of shrivelled sweetness. As per Brotto's instructions, I looked at it in my hand as though I were discovering it for the very first time. I moved it between my fingers, taking in its crinkly skin and dark maroon exterior. I squished it between my thumb and forefinger before pressing it up to my nose and inhaling deeply. It smelled sweet, in a musty sort of way, as dried fruit always does. I allowed my mouth to salivate in eager anticipation, pressing it up against my lips while my tummy rumbled audibly. Finally, when I felt as though there was nothing on this planet I wanted more than this goddam raisin, I popped it into my mouth like a glacé cherry from atop an ice cream sundae, swirling it around in a pool of my own saliva. Pushing it to the roof of my mouth, I caressed its wrinkly skin with my tongue before crushing it into a satisfying little clump of sugar between my teeth. Pleasure flooded through my body instantly. Surely I had never tasted anything so sweet. Nor anything so very delicious. I held the now disintegrated pieces of raisin skin in my mouth for as long as I could, before eventually swallowing everything in one giant gulp, relishing the aftertaste as it lingered generously in my still-salivating palate.

Did I feel more mindful (more demure?) − I think so. I certainly felt notably more aware of the sensations in my body, not least the pleasure this singular raisin had given me.

And that, of course, is the point. Arousal depends more on the mind than it does the body, and when the mind is permanently fragmented because of an onslaught of notifications, tabs, feeds and alerts, staying present in your body long enough to feel sexual sensations is hard. Because pleasure doesn't thrive in our age of distraction. It requires presence, slowness and a willingness to stay with a feeling long enough for it to deepen.

We talk often about sexual freedom now, but rarely about sexual presence. Because while we've never had more options when it comes to swiping, matching and accessing other bodies, the ability to stay attuned and connected during intimacy has never felt harder. And so, deepening our relationship to pleasure is not just about having better sex, it's about cultivating a capacity to stay anchored in our bodies in a world that constantly pulls us away from them. It's about relearning how to inhabit ourselves when the proliferation of digital intimacy trains us to hover between our head and our screen. To be 5ft to the left and unhappy.

In 'Goodbye to All That' (1968), Joan Didion describes how she loved New York 'the way you love the first person who ever touches you and never love anyone quite the same way again.' I've thought about this line often, as I've thought about Library Boy frequently in the eight or so years that have passed since we were together. Several break-ups punctuated our six years as a couple. There have been more attempts at getting back together after The Break-Up than I care to remember. We loved each other, but hurt each other repeatedly over time, as people in love often do. I wasn't sure I could ever love anyone quite so much, but perhaps that's just the way it goes with first loves. Perhaps there is a certain sanctity in them because it's unspoiled. The more times you have your heart broken, the more dangerous and uncontrollable love seems. As author Simon Sinek notes: 'Love is giving someone the power to destroy us and trusting they won't use it'[46]. And yet, invariably, they do.

It has been 14 years since Library Boy and I met on that chilly Manchester morning. He was always so sure of us, at least in the latter half of the relationship, while I grew greedy for more. And dating apps gave me more, at least when it came to romantic options. They gave me access to an infinite supply of great to seemingly unhinged men and allowed me to meet numerous people whose paths I would never ordinarily cross. Perhaps sometimes, admittedly, for good reason. There *is* a limit to my curiosity. But everything comes at a cost, and choosing the *possibility* of everyone ultimately means opting for no one at all. I have continued to question that break-up more than any decision I've made since.

In the years that followed my move to New York, I found the next great love of my life: my best friend, Elspeth. Perhaps because ours is a relationship forever unburdened by the pressures of romance and the timeline of marital expectation, I have found a certain freedom amid the intensity of our platonic partnership. One that has assuaged my mounting commitment phobia, all while teaching me a great lesson in the art of commitment. Alongside Elspeth, my best friend, business partner (for a time) and long-time housemate, I learned how worthwhile are the trade-offs we must make for the sake of relationships. And the responsibility that comes with any admission of love. Ours was not a platonic romance I ever wanted to grow apart from.

Relationships are wonderful, and they are hard. They require constant communication and, sometimes, hard conversations you'd really rather not have. Occasionally, the other person may seem so unreasonable, so deluded in the story they tell themselves, that the relationship feels doomed. You begin to imagine the possibility of all the other lives you might otherwise live, if only with someone else by your side. But whoever you choose to walk through life with, whether a friend or a lover, they are always going to come with baggage. It's just about deciding whose baggage you're willing to take on. So, while dating apps aren't inherently good or bad – they are simply another means by which we can find a partner, or sex – they create a problem for me I simply cannot square.

Insofar as they reinforce the idea that there is always the possibility of something better just a few swipes and clicks away, they have raised my intolerance for everything and anything that seems at odds with the ideal of what I think I'm looking for in love. Moreover, the perception of abundant options has made everyone feel so . . . disposable.

For a time, I found it easier to stay camped out with a WhatsApp boyfriend or two in a purely digital terrain because it meant I didn't have to face the reality that there is no such thing as perfect. I could fall in love, again and again, with the 'avatar in my head'. But what a waste.

And so, one day in the months following sex therapy, I reached for my phone, and rather than open a dating app, I deleted them all instead. The work I needed to do outside of the therapy room was not to swipe more in search of WhatsApp lovers, but to go deeper in my exploration of my body and its sensations. To expose myself to the vulnerability of real, unguarded intimacy. And to learn the dance of connection with a fallible stranger, as flawed and imperfect as me. Sometimes, apparently, it starts with a raisin.

## Chapter 9

# The Sexual Healer

The sun was shining as I sped through the Portuguese countryside on a tightly packed train. It was early spring, and the air was warm, my cotton dress loose enough for the breeze to tickle my body as I swayed, clutching the pole in the middle of the carriage. I was deep in thought. What would he be like, I wondered? We had spoken on Zoom a week before I travelled to Lisbon, to introduce ourselves and discuss our first meeting. He was old(ish), probably in his early sixties, and had a tight grey bun on the top of his head, crowning a perfectly oval face of taut, tanned skin. He was not *not* good-looking for an older guy, I thought.

This bronzed man who lived on the outskirts of Lisbon was billed, by the numerous women who had recommended him to me, as a sexual healer who could work miracles. One friend in particular, the woman I was staying with at the time, said he had touched her in a way no man had touched her before. She'd spent hours in his studio having her body pressed and massaged, she recounted, while he 'moved energy' around. Then, as he proceeded to the 'internal work', she'd felt some sort of seismic release as she emitted what she could only describe as primal, animalistic groans that sounded otherworldly. My eyes had widened as she'd continued to describe the earth-shattering orgasm she'd then experienced, followed by an energetic shift within her that reverberated around the halls of her body for days. I booked a session that day. I was intrigued.

Sex therapy had given me a new language with which to think about my body, and the confidence to explore what I liked and what I wanted more of. But now I was curious to know what a more hands-on, sexological bodywork session might unlock. How it would feel to be called into my body physically with a practitioner, as opposed to simply cognitively through talking therapy.

Before our session, we spoke on Zoom. The Sexual Healer explained to me how he worked – both externally and internally – including the sexual component to his energy work. He wanted to ensure I was comfortable with the physical nature of his practice. I was, I said, noting how unthinkable an experience like this would have been to me months before. Curiosity had replaced shame, and I was hungry to push at the boundaries of my sexual capacity. If only to understand what those boundaries were.

I arrived just after lunch, at around 2pm. The Sexual

Healer opened the door to his flat wearing a long, grey linen tunic and matching trousers, ushering me into what felt like a cavernous den, terracotta sheets hanging from the ceiling and candles burning everywhere I turned. A plume of incense shot up my nose as I followed him into his practice room. The ground was layered with rugs and orange blankets, cushions piled into neat stacks in the four corners. More candles were burning. As we sat down opposite one another on the floor, he opened a big folder and began asking me questions about my relationship to my body, my sexual past, any traumas I felt aware of, all the while jotting down my answers with a stubby pencil. Finally, he told me we were ready to start our bodywork and would I like to go and get changed?

During the hours that followed, I lay flat on my back in just knickers as the Sexual Healer moved from one part of my body to the next, working his way from my feet and ankles, all the way up my legs to my stomach, eventually reaching my head. He pressed down on certain pressure points, asking as he did how every touch felt and what emotions I was experiencing, before eliciting my permission to move on to the next body part. As he dug his thumb into an area near my collarbone, I felt a well of sadness burst inside me; when he moved to an area on my head, I felt rage. With every new touch, a novel feeling was unleashed, and with every request to explain how I felt, what sensations were moving through me, I was called back into my body, forced to be present whenever my mind began to wander.

Eventually, the Sexual Healer arrived at my pelvis and asked again whether I was happy to continue. 'Yes,' I blurted out too quickly. I had come with a purpose, naturally, determined to experience the sort of transcendental orgasm my friend had described, even though I had been strictly instructed to remove all expectations and 'goals' from my mind at the start of the session.

I took off my underwear and lay back down, closing my eyes. The Sexual Healer began to touch the area at the top of my pubic bone above my vulva, before gently moving his fingers down until they were touching the top of my labia. Again he asked if I was happy for him to continue. Again I gave an enthusiastic YES, and he began to massage the area around my clitoris, slowly at first, and then a bit faster with added pressure. He asked whether he could go inside me and with my consent pushed a finger and then two into my vagina, all the while still circling the area around my clitoris. Gently, he began to 'pump' my cervix, as he described it, and the build-up of pressure enveloped me, my body breaking into paroxysms of pleasure, the waves of my orgasm rippling through me from head to toe . . .

. . . and then he touched my foot, and the waves stopped. It was the first time he had touched any part of my body without asking, and suddenly it felt too intimate (it's not lost on me that a touch of my toe felt too much while the man's hand was still up my vagina). I said I was done, and he slid his fingers out of me delicately before draping a blanket across my torso, advising that I continue lying there and allowing the sensations to pulse through me for several minutes longer. When the final orgasmic buzz had ebbed away, I got up and went to get dressed while the Sexual Healer made us both tea. I looked at the clock. Four and a half hours had passed since I'd first stepped into his apartment.

We sat across from one another as we had at the start and, sipping on whatever herbal blend he'd concocted in his glass teapot, he handed me a jar of molasses cookies, their sweetness prickling my tongue deliciously, as though my every nerve ending and taste bud had been brought into new life. He asked how I'd found the experience. What had I liked? Was there anything I didn't like? Had I felt able to articulate my boundaries at every moment? How had my orgasm felt? Was there anything I wanted to discuss before I left? I attempted to distil a smorgasbord of feelings into something resembling a coherent reflection as we dived into our detailed debrief. It was the most present in my body I had felt in a long time, I told him. Perhaps ever. Every time my mind began to wander, his words had brought me out of my head and back into my body.

Finally, I handed him a wad of cash. A rather large wad since it was pay by the hour and, well, many an hour had passed by the time we were bidding our goodbyes. *The most expensive orgasm of my life*, I thought, as I stepped out into the cool evening air. An electric current was moving through my body – an echo of the orgasm that had proven so all-encompassing. I walked back to the station and boarded the next train to the city.

# The most expensive orgasm of my life

The following evening I went for dinner with a group of friends. I told them about the Sexual Healer and the hours I'd spent lying naked on his floor. About the way he'd moved energy around my body and called me into myself in a way I hadn't experienced before. I told them about the orgasm, and the foot. They looked at me bemused. Then one friend asked why I'd paid so much to be fingered. Surely I could have found someone to finger me for free, she wondered? There was no shortage of 10-fingered men jostling around the city looking for sex. She had a point. But this was different, I said, at pains to explain that it wasn't really sex.

It was the first time I'd been in a sensual situation in which I hadn't felt in any way compelled to perform for the other person, nor reciprocate any evocation of my pleasure. In this instance, I had allowed myself simply to receive. And where in the past I had all too often disconnected from my body during intimacy, stepping out of myself as soon as I felt a modicum of discomfort, anxiety or even boredom, the Sexual Healer's stream of questions as he moved across my torso kept me present.

I leaned back and thought about this. I have never really considered how my body feels when being touched by someone else, I told the group. I have always focused my attention on how the person doing the touching is feeling and what I think they need from me, how they want to see my body respond. It was confronting to spend hours being touched by someone in a context in which I couldn't be passive, but instead had to articulate what every new sensation evoked in me. It meant I actually had to think about it. Although I regretted not telling him how much I'd disliked him touching my foot. It was the only time during those four or more hours where I had prioritised the Sexual Healer's comfort over my own. Still, I reasoned, the fact I could recognise that an unspoken boundary had been crossed was progress. I had moved one step away from my usual passive tolerance.

'So, was it worth the money?' another friend asked.

Yes, I concluded. It was worth it for how it reintroduced me to my body's boundaries. And because it allowed me to receive pleasure without guilt or shame or a sense of indebtedness. I felt powerful knowing I would pay at the end. It made the transactional nature of the encounter clear. Besides, if I needed a reminder of how differently I felt in my body now versus before sex therapy, this was it.

## 'Let the soft animal of your body love what it loves'

Over the months I had worked with Aleks, things started to shift. Chief among them was how I felt in my body. I'd been learning how to view my body differently. To spend time with it in a way that felt pleasurable rather than punitive. And to view it with a less critical lens any time I looked in the mirror. Rather than glaring at my reflection and zooming in on every small perceived change – a pinch of extra fat here; a bit of bloat there; less definition around the jawline – instead I'd made a practice of listing off things I liked.

It was the sort of exercise I'd previously considered pointless, and the trademark of some insufferable sort of self-love programme that suggests you can will yourself to love the body you have, or else love yourself to the body you want. Either way, I'd been sceptical and preferred the cool sidelines of vitriolic self-hatred. But there was a limit to where I could go from there. And a limit to what I could experience. Self-hatred and body enmity sucked a lot of time, headspace and energy that had suddenly started to feel like a precious resource I needed to grab back. So, every morning as I reviewed my reflection in the bathroom mirror, I observed several things that, all in all, weren't so bad. In fact, perhaps those things were actually pretty glorious.

I recently interviewed author Sophie Gilbert about her aforementioned book *Girl on Girl*, and when reflecting on the effect her total immersion into toxic noughties pop culture ultimately had on her, she said something that struck me. Like me, she couldn't remember a time when she didn't have a voice in her head reminding her about her weight, telling her she was fat and unattractive – all the horrible things. But dissecting the milieu of misogynistic messaging that defined the cultural landscape of that period, she realised the voice in her head wasn't her own: it was learned. It was the inevitable byproduct of a culture bent on convincing women that our worth exists solely in our looks and our sex appeal, all while reinforcing an impossible beauty ideal we are universally supposed to pursue.

As Simone de Beauvoir observed: 'One is not born but becomes a woman.' We are cultured into believing that we are forever in this state of becoming. Never quite enough as we are, but constantly in need of improvement just to exist. Within this vanity economy the beauty industry creates, we are taught to believe that our bodies are projects that must be worked on. Construction sites that'll never be finished. But Gilbert felt relieved when she recognised it was a learned voice and could therefore be unlearned. No more becoming; just being. I, too, had begun that process of unlearning, shedding skin that now felt heavy. Dispelling the myths that overran my garden.

The second shift I had noticed was in how I felt I should treat my body. In learning to 'seduce myself', I had learned in turn to care for myself. Any time I'd felt that familiar rush of shame and guilt following a meal, then found myself like clockwork heading to the toilet to stick two fingers down my throat in order to throw it up, I'd stop, thinking about Aleks's caution: that for as long as I stayed at war with my body, I would struggle to enjoy sexual pleasure. There was something so particularly grotesque about the very visceral emblem of body war that purging represented. It suddenly felt so aggressive. So harmful.

What had it felt like before, if not aggressive, I wondered? Like a reset, I suppose. Like turning back the clock on a perceived moment of gluttony. But I no longer felt such a strong compulsion to turn backwards, nor so obsessive a focus on resisting my own greed. Naomi Wolf's words rang in my ears. 'Women are insatiable,' she wrote. 'We are greedy. Our appetites do need to be controlled if things are to stay in place. If the world were ours too, if we believed we could get away with it, we would ask for more love, more sex, more money, more commitment to children, more food, more care. These sexual, emotional, and physical demands would begin to extend to social demands: payment for care of the elderly, parental leave, childcare, etc. The force of female desire would be so great that society would truly have to reckon with what women want, in bed and in the world.' I willed myself to rediscover a modicum of the greed I'd learned over the years to suppress. To nurture rather than quash the desires and longings from which that greed sprung.

The third shift was perhaps the more obvious one. When I'd first arrived in Aleks's virtual therapy room, ill-equipped and unwilling to speak openly about sex, least of all any specific challenges I faced in relation to it, now I was fascinated by the topic. Fascinated by what my connection to sex and pleasure revealed about my relationship to myself and to my body. More so by what the list of sex myths I had compiled during our sessions showed me about our wider sex culture. Particularly, I thought, the ways in which, to borrow Anna Carson's phrase again, a door had been placed on women's mouths. Silencing our words and cutting us off from our bodies. When we are disconnected from our sexuality, we are disconnected from our bodies and hence cut off from a critical part of ourselves. How many women have been shamed out of their pleasure, I wondered?

I read once that our capacity to talk about sex is like a muscle: the more we exercise it, the better we get at using it. In an area in which I had always seemed weak, I now felt my strength growing. I was ready to flex my muscles. The more I talked about sex, the more my shame around the topic seemed to dissipate. Falling from the bone like tender meat.

In my final session with Aleks, I told her how much our conversations had changed the way I saw my body. How I'd turned up to our first Zoom room thinking we'd talk about masturbating techniques for an hour and be done with it. And then the relief I'd felt when she'd asked me about my body. Before then, I'd always spoken about my eating disorder as something from the past. This thing that had happened to me in my teens, but from which I now had critical distance. That initial session was the first time I'd really admitted, as much to myself as to anyone else, that I was still on the edges of the maelstrom. Circling this illness that had forever gnawed at the corners of my mind, creating a rupture between self and body. I didn't know then that making peace with my body would be the first step towards my sexual healing, but now it seemed so obvious and necessary a place to begin.

Aleks smiled and told me about a poem she'd recently come across by Mary Oliver called 'Wild Geese'. 'It made me cry,' she said. 'This body is so precious. You only get one, and it's not perfect, but it has to be perfect enough for you, because you have no choice. And so if it wants to eat the damn pasta, let it eat the damn pasta. And if it needs to rest, then let it rest. And if it needs to cry, then let it cry. And if it needs to dance, then let it dance. It is a precious gift to have a body and to be able to build a relationship with your body where you become friends. If you can live your life in that friendship and it not be so conflicted and distressing, then the rest is easy.'

*The rest is easy.*

After we spoke I looked up Oliver's poem, noting that before the poet addresses the body, she writes that 'you' (me? You? All womankind?) 'do not have to be good'. Nor, she says, must we spend our lives repenting. I read that first line as: you don't have to be a *good girl.* Society conditions young women to believe we must be perfect in order to be acceptable and to be compliant in order to be liked. Our connection to sexuality invariably becomes entangled in this dictate as we are taught that our bodies are always in service of others. Through the many myths that get layered onto our understanding of sex, we are led to believe that how we choose to explore our sexuality has some wider meaning and implication beyond the sheer enjoyment and pleasure this exploration may give us. That sex is a gift we must bestow upon someone the first time, after which our worth diminishes. That there is an endless list of rules around what it means to do sex right. No sex on the first date, only on the third. Have casual sex. Don't have casual sex. Don't be a slut. But don't you dare be a prude.

'Question everything,' Aleks reminded me. 'Take a critical approach to whenever "should" comes up in your connection to sex: *I should have sex like this. I should orgasm like that.* Question it all, and interrogate who benefits (i.e. makes money) from you hating your body or your face. You do not have to repent for who you are even if the world is constantly telling you you need to be different. You do not have to be "good" in accordance with anyone else's standards.'

As we started to wrap up our final session, I told her I liked sex therapy because, at least in my case, there was a clear metric for success. I started out unable to orgasm, and now I could come again. Where other therapeutic disciplines, with their focus on parental relationships and childhood trauma, had lost me early on because they seemed slow at getting to the point, the impact of sex therapy was more immediately tangible. But Aleks pushed back. The work we did together was never just about my being able to orgasm or not. It was about shifting my perspective on my body, from distrusting it and criticising it, to learning to advocate for what I wanted. One of the benefits of this process was that it allowed me to feel less anxious during sex, to experience more desire and ultimately to be able to orgasm. But that was never the point of the work. And nor was it the end.

Years later, I understood what she meant: that the goal was not to learn how to have better sex, but to reconcile with my body for the sake of no longer living in opposition to myself. As much as my productivity-addled brain sought tangible ways through which I could measure progress in our sessions through improvements in my sex life, that was just the start. I peeled back the first layer of shame and found myself able to say, 'Touch me there!', but there were many more layers to go.

## Odd woman in Rome, self-romancing, eating pasta

I wanted to celebrate, to do something to mark this turning over of a new sexual leaf, so I booked my first solo trip away. To the romantic capital of the world no less: Rome. My own *Eat Pray Love* moment beckoned, and what better way to continue seducing myself than with several days drinking wine al fresco and marvelling at Caravaggio's eroticised Madonna at the Borghese? Like a good student, I took with me a fresh copy of Esther Perel's *Mating in Captivity* (2006) and a brand new Moleskin, ready to begin writing about this fresh chapter in my life.

In the days that followed, I moved through the city with a lightness of being that would have made Kundera proud. I started each day with a hot coffee and pastry from the bakery just a few blocks from where I was staying and wandered to the local piazza to dip flaky pieces of croissant into the warm liquid while the church bells rang. Delirious from my sugar high, I'd spend the following hours wandering the city like a true flâneuse, imagining myself the Vivian Gornick of Rome as I drank in the crowds bathed in sunshine and daydreamed about the future. As the city grew dark, I'd look for the best restaurant in whatever area I found myself, and sit for the evening writing about my day while forking giant pieces of aubergine parmigiana into my mouth, reassuring the waiters that, no, I was not waiting for anyone else to arrive and, no, I did not need a tour guide for the remainder of my stay. I was so perfectly content alone.

By day three, I had filled half my notebook. In one entry I described a ravioli-making class I attended near the Vatican, which was led by a woman called Romana who ran a coffee shop called Mr Coffee and Mrs Cake. After crafting delicate little cheese bundles to throw into a giant pot, my fellow pasta-making students and I gathered around the dinner table where we devoured our creations alongside a bottle of prosecco. It was the first time I'd eaten pasta since I was 13 years old. Another entry consisted of hastily scribbled notes from a tarot card reading, given to me by a woman who had recently returned to Rome for love. Among the cards she drew from the deck was the Death card, which apparently signified that I needed to rid myself of the debris in my life. 'Pull down the trees that have already yielded their fruit,' she advised, and make way for new crops. Her mixing of metaphors aside, the message to me felt clear: keep shedding that old skin.

Periodically, I turned my attention to the contents of Perel's *Mating in Captivity*, specifically to the idea of eroticism. It was a concept that had captured my imagination for the duration of the trip, providing the lens through which I'd begun to see myself savouring every taste, every painting, every view. Perel had taken what seemed at first unlikely inspiration for her exploration of the erotic: her parents. They were Holocaust survivors, she wrote, whose disposition on life following the unimaginable had distinguished them from many of their friends – friends who were divided into two different tranches. On one side were those who were alive because they didn't die and who now moved through life in a kind of emotional survival mode. On the other side were those who were alive because they chose to live and had henceforth committed themselves to living life to the fullest – seeking out pleasure, beauty and joy in every moment.

That Perel's parents never talked about *why* they survived, but only about the way they wanted *to live* after they survived, encapsulated for her the essence of eroticism. It is never just about sex, she writes, but instead about imagination, creativity, sensuality and the life force that animates desire – 'the erotic is the antidote to death.' I copied the quote onto the middle of a single page in my notebook and underlined it several times, thinking back to what Seema had said to me about pleasure being the counter to apathy. 'Our relationship to sex is never just about fucking,' I wrote on the following page. 'It's about how we relate to ourselves: to our bodies, our desires, our pleasure. It's about our capacity for vulnerability; our ability to ask for what we want and our willingness to communicate what it is that we need.' We miss out on a lot, I thought, when we are taught to live in opposition to our needs instead of in communion with them.

Did I know what I wanted now?

I wasn't sure. But I felt the rumblings of a hunger I had

hitherto learned to suppress. The imperative to reach out in search of more. More experiences, more sensuality, more sustenance, *more pleasure*. Was this the life force Perel referred to? The drive to desire and then be led by those desires? Yes.

# THREE YEARS LATER

## The Priest and the Sinner –
## My (Re) Introduction to Porn

One balmy evening during a late London summer, I joined the end of a long queue that snaked out of the doors at Dalston Rio, spilling eager cinemagoers out onto the street and into the waning sunshine. It was the busiest I'd seen any movie theatre in years. Peering in, I could make out hordes of people flocked around the bar as the popcorn machine whirred and a member of staff shook their cocktail shaker exaggeratedly. There was a buzz in the air. It's not every night you get to watch porn in the cinema, but tonight we were all here for a screening hosted by feminist filmmaker Erika Lust. The evening marked the 20-year anniversary of Lust Films, Erika's porn production company.

Clutching a bag of popcorn and a freshly made margarita, I walked into the screening room where I recognised a line of sex educators, writers and performers taking their seats and joined them at the front, eager not to sit alone for my first erotic movie night. The lights dimmed, and where credits would typically begin to roll, instead Erika took to the stage to introduce the evening's viewing. We were going to be shown a montage of some of her favourite films from over the past two decades, Lust told us, starting with the first porn film she ever made: *The Good Girl*, a 'pizza delivery boy' porn cliché but filmed from the perspective of the woman. I nervously shoved popcorn into my mouth as the screen flickered into life, and we were transported to a quintessential European flat where a woman was rushing to do up her dressing gown as the doorbell rang. The pizza was here!

There followed a film set in a church where performer Calita Fire was sitting in the confessional booth asking for a priest's forgiveness. She had sinned, she said. She was guilty of lust. Lust for a man she could not have. Lust for a man who had given himself to God. The *Fleabag* aficionados among us grew hot under the collar, more so when the film jumped to the priest committing that most (un)holy of acts with his confessor among the pews.

The film cut and suddenly we were by a pool with performer Kazumi, who licked a lollipop on a sweltering hot summer's day. Here we were given a behind-the-scenes look into how the concept for the film, a gangbang by the pool, was first conceived. It was Kazumi's idea, it transpired, and at first Lust resisted. 'How could a gangbang be feminist?' she wonders aloud. 'A woman wouldn't want a group of men to all take their turn with her, would she? It would be objectifying!' But that's exactly what Kazumi wanted. She wanted to be the centre of attention amongst a group of hot, sweating men as they lavished her body and fucked her from every angle. Lust relented, and so the camera followed her around the set as she talked to the performers and crew about how they planned on translating Kazumi's fantasy into reality, but through the female perspective.

It had been several years since I'd first started sex therapy, and my curiosity about sex and pleasure had extended beyond the limits of my own body. When Aleks and I had wrapped up our sessions together, it felt as though I'd only just peeled back the first layer on a topic I was now fascinated by. I no longer felt broken, but I didn't feel 'fixed' either, chiefly because I wasn't convinced there was any end goal of sexual enlightenment I was now working towards. The work, it seemed, was to continue probing the different facets of my sexual experience as my body changed and evolved, and as I started to learn more about what I liked.

It seemed increasingly strange to me now that our wider cultural conversations around sex remained so limited. Reduced to performance or marketing spiel, and all the while devoid of the depth and texture I'd come to appreciate in my conversations with Aleks. I'd learned firsthand that how we connect to our bodies and how we experience pleasure is a fundamental part of what it means to be alive. And yet I continued to meet women who felt as I once did: broken in their relationship to sex and disconnected from their pleasure. So I decided to follow in the footsteps of my self-pleasure icon, Betty Dodson, and bring together groups of women to sit shoulder to shoulder and discuss the very things we'd all been conditioned not to address. To talk about sex, bodies, pleasure, intimacy, desire and all the things that shape it. Fix the system, not the women, as Laura Bates says. But first, we need to understand how exactly the system is fucking us when it comes to the way we experience our bodies. I invited experts working across the sex and pleasure space to come and share their knowledge with us too, titling the series Sex Talks. Why beat around the bush? I reasoned. At the end of every talk I asked the audience to submit their anonymous sex questions via pen and paper, receiving a mountainous stack of questions every time. As it turned out, people had just as many unanswered thoughts around the topic as I once had.

One of the subjects we returned to repeatedly at Sex Talks was porn. Unsurprising, given how pervasive and accessible porn has become in today's world. It doesn't matter whether you choose to watch it yourself, because undoubtedly some of the people you sleep with have or do. And it continues to shape our wider sexual landscape regardless – for good and for bad. Often, people think bad. But when I interviewed the likes of Erika Lust and other independent creators and performers working in the space, I began to think differently. Recognising a nuance I hadn't appreciated previously because I had seen porn as a monolith, one giant projection of everything I'd ever guiltily scrolled past on RedTube or

PornHub. One huge performance that re-entrenched a narrow view of sex devoid of pleasure, and pleasure solely in service of the male gaze.

I didn't grow up watching porn, chiefly because I thought porn was bad. I believed that it was inherently misogynistic, and if I watched it then I'd be contributing in my own small way to the broader oppression of women. When my first boyfriend admitted that he'd started watching porn at eight years old, I was horrified. It hadn't so much as featured as a topic of conversation among my friends at school, let alone a group viewing activity. To think of him as a child watching people have sex, before he even really understood what sex was, felt disturbing. It reconfirmed my worst suspicions about what I saw as the dark underbelly of the World Wide Web.

But more recently I'd grown curious as to what 'feminist' porn might be able to teach me and others about the nuances of eroticism and the variety of sexual exploration. I wondered what role films like the ones Lust makes could play in shaping a more female-pleasure-centric sexual economy. Or whether this was another iteration of performance I'd really rather avoid. When I asked Lust about creating porn through a feminist lens, and how different it made the end-product from what was otherwise available on mainstream sites, her response was to compare the two experiences to different dining options. Opting for free porn on the tube sites is like going to get fast food, she said, while paying for something on her own platform, or another independent site, was akin to going to a family-run business. Everything is food, at the end of the day, but what the chefs do with their ingredients in each establishment is very different.

'The ready availability of free, fast-food porn is a problem,' Lust said, riddled as it is with the sexualisation of teens, systemic violence towards women, and racism. 'But it's not only in the porn world,' she told me. 'This is happening on other platforms too. It's happening in the music world, on Instagram, on mainstream television platforms.' Porn holds a mirror up to society, magnifying issues that are already deeply embedded in our culture. But it's possible to do things differently. 'Porn can be educational, artistic, and cinematic. It can help us to tell stories about how people relate to each other sexually, how we communicate, how we negotiate our boundaries, how we can talk about consent. It can be a tool for excitement, to empower ourselves and our own sexuality, to explore who we want to be in our own desires and fantasies. I think it has this huge potential, but it's been so taboo. For so many people, it's still so stigmatised.'

Erotic material always has been.

## Can I watch porn and still be a feminist?

In 1959, Britain introduced the Obscene Publications Act, which made it illegal to publish anything thought to 'deprave and corrupt' – although what was considered 'obscene' was the subject of much debate. It was typified by a landmark court case involving a novel the prosecution described as likely to 'induce lustful thoughts in the minds of those who read it'. The book? *Lady Chatterley's Lover*, which follows a woman who, desperate for sexual connection after her husband is paralysed during the war, turns to her gamekeeper, Oliver Mellors, to satiate her needs. Author D. H. Lawrence described the book as part of his 'labour [to] make the sex relations valid and precious, instead of shameful.' A man after my own heart. But the British Crown, represented by prosecutor Mervyn Griffith-Jones, tried to stop the book from being published under the aforementioned Act, bringing charges against the publisher, Penguin Books. It wasn't just the book's 13 sex scenes that so disturbed them. 'The word "fuck" or "fucking" appears no less than 30 times . . .' Griffith-Jones lamented. 'While "cunt" 14 times; "balls" 13 times; "shit" and "arse" six times apiece; "cock" four times; "piss" three times, and so on.' Scandalous.

In the end, it took just three hours for the jury to unanimously declare Penguin Books *not* guilty of disseminating an obscene publication. Just one month later, the book sold some 2 million copies nationwide, making this story the perfect vignette for what has always been true when it comes to erotic content in its ever-evolving guises: many people want to consume it. Some people want to suppress it.

Britain was already on the cusp of social change, and the decade that followed this scintillating public scandal saw the introduction of a swath of liberalising laws that made abortion permissible under certain circumstances, divorce easier, and which decriminalised homosexuality. In his poem 'Annus

Mirabilis', Philip Larkin branded 1963 'the miracle year', when the lifting of the *Lady Chatterley's Lover* book ban and the release of the Beatles's first LP signified that finally, sex had become (at least somewhat) culturally permissible.

But the landscape of erotic content we're surrounded by today is worlds away from what was available during this decade of liberalisation, and different even from what was available just 20 or so years ago. This, of course, is thanks to the birth of the internet and, in no small part, to one man: Fabian Thylmann. Thylmann is often credited with revolutionising (and destabilising) the porn industry after he bought up a bunch of major adult sites – including Pornhub, YouPorn, RedTube and Brazzers – under his company Manwin (later renamed MindGeek and more recently Aylo). By making porn free to access and ad-supported, he transformed how adult content was produced, distributed and consumed, heralding the start of the fast-food free-streaming era with which Lust takes issue. Today, Pornhub gets billions of visits per month, and 13 years old is the average age a child in the UK first sees porn, although 10% of children have viewed it by age nine.

On Holloway Road in London's Islington, there's a small shop with blacked-out windows called We Buy Any Porn. It's a hard place to visit because it's only open on Tuesdays and Fridays between 12pm and 6pm, but stepping inside this little erotic enclave is like entering a sex-world time machine. Lining the walls are shelves stacked high with old porn magazines, erotic books, naked postcards and any other old-school porn memorabilia you can imagine. From archaic *Playboy* magazines to niche erotic journals, the variety of porn literature is vast. I used to live nearby and went to browse its towers of analogue porn mags a few times. Between photos of women with big bushes and even bigger boobs, and muscly men with bulging . . . ambitions, there were magazines showcasing essays on topics like the release of controversial 70s porn film *Deep Throat*, the tension around sex within feminism, and the moral crusades against porn. It struck me every time I ventured into this little vestige from the past just how different an experience it was consuming erotic content in this way. How much slower and less titillating than what has been normalised online in today's shock economy, where platforms competing for our attention are becoming increasingly extreme. Anything to keep us watching.

On the few(ish) occasions I've turned to a free porn site for a quick hit, I've felt seedy and gross scrolling through videos boasting 'young teen girls', violent gangbangs and MILFs. I've always veered towards lesbian massage porn because it seemed the most sensual and least violent of what was on offer, but the videos are still punctuated by pop-ups showing young women having come squirted onto their faces, or else someone being choked by a giant penis, and they're always surrounded by ads for more extreme videos. Everyone's sexual preferences are different, but the whole viewing experience makes me uneasy. I'll generally come within about 30 seconds, and then questions will ping around my head: *Did the porn performers want to be there? Were they being paid properly? Did that woman in the sidebar like being strangled? Can I watch porn and still be a feminist?*

It was this latter question that was front of mind when I sat in the Dalston Rio surrounded by a sea of journalists and watched a montage of Lust's erotic back catalogue. Because in Lust's world, the answer is a resounding *yes*. The key is to pay for your porn on platforms that you know pay performers properly, prioritise female pleasure and are inclusive of different sexualities, genders and body types. And Lust's cinematic sex scenes don't disappoint. I wondered as I watched just how different my relationship to sex would have been if I'd grown up exposed to this sort of porn. To videos that demonstrated what sensuality looked like, how different everyone's bodies, and specifically our genitals, truly are, and how varied are the ways in which we can have sex. And I wondered what difference it would have made if the men I'd slept with had watched films that focused on women's pleasure. Films in which the clitoris took centre stage rather than a thrusting dick, and in which a woman's orgasm wasn't just an afterthought, but the main event. Would they have approached the sex we'd had differently? Would I?

When journalist Jon Ronson was finishing *So You've Been Publicly Shamed* (2015), he set up an interview with porn performer Princess Donna about how free, pirated distribution was reshaping the industry. On the afternoon of their interview, he headed down to the hotel lobby at the Chateau Marmont in Los Angeles and was met by a woman dressed, he said, 'like a mad peacock'. In her tight, bright dress, she stood out among a sea of grey and blue hoodies. As Ronson walked towards her, he noticed a flicker of contempt move across the hotel receptionist's face. It struck him that this man might happily watch porn in private, yet in public looked down on the performer in front of him. That moment became the catalyst for Ronson's deep dive into the world of porn in his audio series *The Butterfly Effect*, in which he sets out to better understand the lives of performers and the stigma they face. Sitting in the cinema, I thought about what that look had revealed to Ronson about one man's biases around porn. And then I thought about my own. I decided, if I was to understand the nuances of so-called 'feminist' porn and what it might be able to teach me about pleasure, I should probably visit a feminist porn set and speak to the performers myself.

## Me, the mums making porn, and a foursome

Six months later, I flew to Barcelona, where Erika Lust's production team is based. It was my fourth or fifth time in the city, but it never seemed to get any more familiar. Or maybe I just felt like a different person every time I returned. I wanted to know more about the people who performed pleasure for the camera. I wanted to see what it could look like to create porn in which women's pleasure was prioritised. And I wanted to explore what it would feel like to be so close to other people's sexuality when I had, for so long, felt so distant from my own.

I had been speaking to Lust's team for a while now trying to figure out the best time to visit, since their production schedule changed constantly. But now the stars were aligned, and there were five shoots happening in quick succession, all of which I was invited to sit in on. I booked my flights immediately, and on the plane I started writing a long list of questions to ask the performers and crew. I arrived just in time for the start of anal season.

My first day on set started early. The shoot took place in a giant warehouse on the edge of the city, and I decided to walk there to clear my head. I left my hotel at the crack of dawn and strolled the 40 or so minutes to get there with a coffee in hand. This has always been my favourite time of day in any new city – right on the cusp of people beginning their morning, when there is a calm sleepiness blanketing otherwise bustling streets and the frenzy of the night before has been swept away. The sun was beginning to edge over the horizon when I got to the studio, drenching the surrounding buildings in the warm morning light, while the streets behind stayed chilly in the shadows. I buzzed the door and waited for someone to let me in.

The studio was alive with busy crew members when I walked up to the green room. They had to build the set from scratch, the director told me, so the production team had been deep in construction mode for several hours already. I refilled my cup with more coffee and headed upstairs to meet the intimacy co-ordinator – a woman called Annarella, who used to be a porn performer herself but now worked semi-regularly on Lust's productions. Her role was to make sure everyone's boundaries were made clear before each shoot, and then respected during filming. She can call 'cut' if anyone looks uncomfortable.

Otherwise, Lust's team tends not to intervene too much once the cameras are rolling, the producer told me. Performers are given the outline for a scene, advised on any specific positions or vignettes the director wants to capture, and then pretty much left to enjoy having sex the way they want to. The director will interrupt things only in pretty rare cases, she said, like when someone squirted all over the camera and they had to take a pause to clean the screen.

I watched as one of the performers had her photograph taken. She was wearing a sheer pink cape and matching under-wear, and looked ethereal in soft, dewy makeup with her pixie-cut hair. Her name was Hannah, and she had just flown in from Berlin. This was her first time working on a Lust production, although she had been doing sex work for a while. I asked her why she had first started working in porn, and she said sex had always felt like a performance for her. Growing up, she said she'd constantly felt sexualised by men but like there was never any space for her to express her own sexuality or desires on her terms. 'It's always about what men perceive or want from sex.'

And so, she'd started experimenting with amateur porn a few years ago, filming things with friends, mainly women, as a way of exploring her body and ridding herself of sexual shame. She had grown up a Jehovah's Witness, believing she shouldn't have sex before marriage, and spent her entire childhood feeling as though someone was watching her, ready to pounce if she did anything bad. Eventually she left the church and started to explore kink and BDSM in her twenties, before moving on to porn. For the first time, she said, she could explore her fantasies, get to know – even like – her body, and see her sexuality as something exciting rather than frightening; something for herself rather than for someone else.

As it turned out, she was really turned on by being filmed. 'I want people to talk about their deepest, darkest fantasies,' she told me. 'Because if you don't, they get repressed – and that turns into shame. But if you say them out loud, play with them, even laugh about them, they lose their power. Your fantasies don't define you; they're just stories your mind tells to release something.' I thought back to a recent interview I'd hosted for Sex Talks discussing a little postcard book called *Sex Secrets* (2022) by Eleanor Tattersfield.

Following the success of her first book, *Lockdown Secrets* (2021), she'd put out a call on social media for people to send in their deepest, darkest, funniest sex secrets by way of anonymous postcards, and was inundated with responses. Together, they painted a tapestry of a broad variety of sexual fantasies accompanied by a pretty universal experience of sexual shame. One man had written in saying: 'I asked my wife to peg me. She said no. Now we can't look each other in the eye.'

I picked up my notebook and pen to head downstairs to the studio and bumped into Jimmy, one of the male performers, en route. He was standing at the top of the stairs looking over the balcony at the scene below, his dressing gown loose across his body. As I walked up to join him, he turned around to return my hello, seemingly indifferent to the fact that his giant, erect penis was sticking out from beneath his robe. I tried not to look down as we exchanged pleasantries, then someone called his name.

I followed him downstairs and took my seat behind the director, producer and intimacy co-ordinator − all of them women − while he joined Hannah by a king-sized mattress on the floor. The room was bathed in a cool blue light. The entire crew, also composed primarily of women around my age, wore T-shirts emblazoned with Lust's company motto: Own Your Pleasure. Some wore caps to match. Everyone took their positions, and the cameras started rolling.

I was surprised by how normal it felt watching two people have sex, specifically anal sex. I had never so much as entertained a butt plug, so it felt like a comprehensive introduction to the art of butt play. I thought I'd find the experience more titillating, perhaps even shocking, and that would keep me enthralled. But instead it just felt like being on any other shoot, except with a lot more on-screen nakedness. I liked listening to the women in front of me point out how beautiful certain angles were, noting the lighting, the performer's positioning, the cinematography. I understood then what Hannah had meant when she'd described the porn she made as art − something she did because it was beautiful, aesthetic, even authentic. It was deeply sensual, and I found myself leaning forward in my seat as though at a gallery, trying to take in a sculpture from all its various angles.

What made the scene feel intimate and 'authentic' was also that it was slow – very, very slow – and after some 45 minutes watching the two writhing bodies in front of me manoeuvre into different positions, I started to feel a creeping sense of boredom. I willed one or both performers to orgasm so we could all be released and I could get more coffee and a snack.

Later, Hannah told me that she did indeed have a real orgasm, but reminded me this was not the sole measure of good sex, either on screen or off. I nodded, biting into another slice of cake.

In the days that followed, I watched what felt like a lot of porn – at least for someone seldom in the habit of consuming on-screen erotic content. One film involved two women experimenting with sex and hair. An odd-sounding combination and an equally bizarre thing to watch. Both performers took it in turns to wrap giant plaits of dark brown hair around one another's bodies, occasionally rubbing said plait up and down the other's crotch. Eventually they licked each other out, all while trying to make use of various additional hair props.

Another, Marie Antoinette-inspired film featured a set of brightly coloured cakes bearing slogans like 'Sluts win', 'Let's make out' and, my personal favourite, 'Heartbreaker, butt-fuck lover'. It was anal season after all. Romeo, the male performer, was dressed in a hot-pink apron and chef's hat, while his co-star Kazumi wore sky-high heels and pink lingerie. Her only boundary during the pre-shoot 'sex talk' was that Romeo must not fuck cake into her ass. He gave her his word. When I sat down to talk to Kazumi afterwards, cake remnants were still smeared across the set floor and a streak of icing was encrusted in her hair.

On my final day, Erika herself was directing, which meant the budget was bigger, the studio vast and the production more technical. The set was particularly busy since we were now joined by a documentary crew who were there filming a segment of a forthcoming docu-reality TV show called *Mums Make Porn*. Four Belgium-based mums were on a mission to make ethical, educational porn, and ahead of their debut next month, they wanted to garner some hot tips from Erika on exploring consent and female pleasure on screen.

Since the studio was so busy, no one was allowed to be on set during the sex scene bar the core crew, so the four mums and I were instead crammed into a makeshift viewing room with two large monitors. As we prepared to watch the ensuing foursome, a cameraman zoomed around the room, practising filming the mums from different angles in order to catch their each and every reaction. The show's producer hovered nervously nearby, trying to make sure I didn't feature too prominently in the background of any one shot. Eventually, her concerned glances grew jarring, and I resorted to sitting on a giant neon-green beanbag at the back of the room.

Finally, the performers entered our screens, making their way to the ginormous bed in the centre of the set. There was a sharp intake of breath amid our viewing ensemble and we all leaned forward. I craned my head trying to peer between the shoulders of two of the mums who, as the scene began, broke into intermittent giggles. Occasionally one of them said, 'Consent! Consent!' And the other three all nodded enthusiastically.

The cameraman zoomed in and out, weaving his way around our little room with impressive dexterity. The audio to the sex scene was primarily channelled through several pairs of headphones the mums were passing between one another. But as bodies became entangled and the heat began to rise, the performers' moans and groans and shrieks of pleasure began to waft audibly into our little hideout.

My first thought was that foursomes look logistically complicated. *Quelle surprise.* There were a lot of moving body parts, and they often ended up splitting off into two pairs, with limbs outstretched periodically to connect the fractured quadruplet. My second thought was that it felt sensual rather than performative or rough, like I was watching two couples have sex at someone's house, rather than on a giant triple king-sized bed in a studio, surrounded by lights and cameras and crew. As before, it also seemed to go on for ages, but this time my attention remained hooked. As the performers took it in turns to take centre stage among the others, I marvelled at how delicately they touched one another while forming this human pleasure train. Attention was lavished on the newbie on set, Addis Fouche, as she leaned back against Bishop Black (a non-binary performer based in Berlin whose muscles rippled every time they so much as breathed) and Calita Fire (of Dalston Rio fame) nuzzled into her pussy.

Looking for details I didn't ordinarily expect to see in 'mainstream' porn, I noticed Calita had hair under her arms and pubes that extend beyond her underwear line to the top of her thighs. It's an important detail, she told me after the shoot. She has a 'full bush', not just a 'top bush', and that's become a core part of her 'brand'. She had body hair long before she first started doing porn, she explained, but has made a point of only working with production companies that don't make her shave her bush. That initially ruled out a lot of the bigger, mainstream production companies, because 'there's no way you ever see a hairy armpit there.' I thought about my New Year's resolution from just a few months prior, which declared 2025 'The Year of The Bush', and then down to my comparatively sparse 'top bush', making a mental note to work harder on my vulva rewilding.

Eventually everyone orgasmed, or at least appeared to (not the measure of good sex, as Hannah had reminded me), and the scene came to an end.

## Resurrecting of a feminist prophet

I returned to the green room and thought about the previous few days. How unimaginable this whole experience would have been to me several years ago and how much I now liked spending time with people who wanted to talk about sex and pleasure and bodies. Not as an awkward, taboo topic, but as something worthy of exploration and nuance. On set I was reminded of how important it is that women's pleasure is represented, particularly in a landscape that is otherwise overrun by male-centric ideas of what sex 'should' look like. I'm continually impressed by women like Erika Lust and also Cindy Gallop (founder of the platform 'Make Love Not Porn' – a 'social sex' video-sharing platform that celebrates real-world sex as a counterpoint to porn) for how they're disrupting an industry long dominated by men. Offering representations of bodies and desire that are sensual rather than sensationalist and that show there is a way to create and share porn differently. That there is value in resisting the compulsion to chase ever more extreme portrayals of often violent sex – at a creative level and also at a business level. Lust's production company is valued at $25 million and employs some 40 or so people. There is money to be made in creating porn that centres the female gaze.

I considered the idea of erotic literacy, which Aleks and I discussed during our first session together. Specifically, how ill-equipped so many of us are with the language of our bodies and our fantasies. Here I could see how integral a role erotic storytelling can play in helping us learn about our sexuality. To get comfortable in a space of erotic fantasy.

And yet, a nagging feeling lingered. However positive a portrayal of female pleasure this small pocket of the industry offered, it was wholly unrepresentative of the broader porn space and most of what is considered 'mainstream'. I wanted more of what Lust was creating, but I couldn't ignore the cost of the wider landscape: an economy that profits most reliably from violence, misogyny and the degradation of women.

A quick browse on the current Pornhub homepage and I'm met with a litany of videos showcasing step-sisters and MILFs, 'barely legal' teens and gangbangs in which women are choked and strangled. Sexual fantasy may be a powerful space in which we can press up against the limits of our experience and our pleasure, but insofar as the contentification of our society is pushing everything to become more extreme, how are these fantasies being hardened and darkened by the never-ending carousel of easy-to-access, free-to-consume violent porn that saturates the internet? Desire isn't formed in a vacuum, and porn plays an outsized role in shaping our erotic imagination. Its images don't merely reflect our sexual urges; they produce them, establishing certain kinds of bodies and pleasures as acceptable, others as peripheral. And it's women and people of minority genders that this harms.

A study[47] in 2020 examining depictions of violence across mainstream, heterosexual porn found that 'women were the target of the aggression in 97% of the scenes, and their response to aggression was either neutral or positive and rarely negative.' Men, the research found, were the perpetrators of this aggression in 76% of scenes. In an era in which misogynistic porn is ubiquitous and young people are increasingly learning about sex through what they see online, our sexual culture is being shaped by content that is less about pleasure than it is about male performance and female endurance. Whether you watch extreme porn or not, you're still participating in a sexual economy informed by it.

What's more, according to the Children's Commissioner for England[48], most children who come across porn today aren't actually seeking it out. They stumble across it accidentally, often while using social media or searching for something else, meaning platforms like X and video apps, rather than traditional adult sites, now serve as gateways to children watching porn. The Commissioner warned that this exposure is increasingly happening before puberty, reframing porn not as a teenage rite of passage so much as an unintended consequence of growing up online.

Perhaps it tallies, then, that Andrea Dworkin's work is making a resurgence. Months before she died in April 2005, she reportedly said to journalist Julie Bindel (notably shunned by many feminists today for her anti-trans views) that 'women will come back to feminism, because things are going to get far, far worse.'[49] We have apparently reached that point, and Dworkin has been resurrected as the bold feminist prophet we need to counter a new brand of Tate- and MAGA-inflected misogyny. In 2025, Picador reissued several of her 12 books, suggesting her work was ripe for rediscovery given today's fraught political landscape. Ideas considered extreme, even hateful, at the time of her writing are now being recognised as urgent. (Throughout her entire professional life, Dworkin was derided by the media for supposedly hating men, hating sexual freedom and even hating the left. She was also shunned by pro-sex feminists, who saw her anti-pornography stance as anti-sex, moralistic and a form of censorship that allied her with conservatives. Her appearance, too, was subject to frequent abuse, with one reviewer in the *London Review of Books* noting: 'The way she rants on is of course the give-away symptom of sexual frustration. Clearly she can't be getting enough of it – not surprising for someone overweight and ugly like her!'[50] Charming.)

Long dismissed as hysterical or puritanical, Dworkin is being re-read now because the conditions she warned about have intensified rather than disappeared. Porn is no longer something you must intentionally seek out but instead forms part of the digital backdrop of everyday life. It's a fixture of our virtual world in which misogyny is algorithmically amplified and sexual inequality is sold back to women as choice, even liberation. You don't have to agree with her rejection of all pornography to recognise the problem she named: that a sexual culture built on male desire – on the dominance of, and entitlement to, women's bodies – will struggle to create the conditions in which pleasure can be mutual.

I spent time on Erika Lust's set wanting to understand what her work might teach me about pleasure, and what it means to depict sex through the female gaze. I left convinced that the question was far bigger than the scope of any one filmmaker, but that the work Lust's team are doing offers a valuable blueprint for how we can overturn our male-centric sexual economy. Andrea Dworkin opposed pornography produced under patriarchy on the grounds that it is inherently exploitative – part of a sexual system that eroticises women's subordination and leaves little room for ethical or feminist alternatives. But I disagree. I have to believe that not everything women create under patriarchy is simply a product of oppression or a function of male power.

We can, and we must, rewrite the sexual script. That means more textured portrayals of women's desire, more diverse bodies, and more narratives that centre female interiority rather than erase it. Because as long as the most profitable content remains extreme, misogynistic and engineered for male libidinal consumption, we remain trapped in a visual sexual economy that teaches women their pleasure is a performance, not a birthright. Women are not immune to reproducing misogyny – but neither is everything women create under patriarchy reducible to exploitation. Representations that help women recognise their own desires and feel more at home in their bodies remain one of the few available counters.

Just then, someone called my name to join them on set. I'd agreed to do a quick cameo for the day's shoot – a 60s-themed game show where the contestants ended up in a foursome. It happens to the best of us. The crew needed cheering audience members, so I volunteered. As I took my seat in a yellow suit and hastily applied Twiggy-esque eyeliner, Bishop Black turned to me and winked. 'It always starts with a cameo.'

*Chapter 10*

# I stopped dating for the plot, then the plot thickened

We met at the gym when I approached him to ask whether or not he took creatine. There was no subtext to my query, since I had little desire to date, least of all someone I saw daily while sweating buckets. But I wanted to know how to peak my performance and I liked flexing my new Cross Fit-informed vernacular to anyone who crossed my path. I was in a health-focused, wellness-loving fitness phase and had become quite insufferable. Gym Boy laughed and responded no. He may have given the impression of being a gym bro (all bulging biceps and rippling abs), but he was not in fact fuelled by a diet of bodybuilding supplements. He just liked working out. 'Interesting,' I said, and walked off.

A few weeks later, we struck up conversation again, except this time I had bigger fish to fry than what supplements

I should be taking. I had now become obsessed with falling birth rates and, never shy of sharing too much about whatever topic is high on my mind, I started to unpack the contents of my whirring brain in between rounds of burpees. Whether feigned or otherwise, Gym Boy was sufficiently interested in my topic du jour to continue asking follow-up questions until I'd run out of information to share. A few days later, I slid into his DMs to send him some of the articles I'd mentioned about why so many young women were choosing not to have children (!). He hearted them all, then we agreed to meet for a drink.

We'd only ever seen one another in Lycra, so as I approached him at the bar I felt a wave of relief wash over me. You never know when a Hawaiian shirt, tight trousers and deck shoes are going to be sprung on you, so his black T-shirt and blue jeans were a pleasant surprise. *He's hot*, I thought, and not in a Gymshark-inflected way. We started talking about our respective lives as opposed to the day's news agenda, exchanging the stories that had shaped us as we intermittently swapped notes on who was reportedly fucking who at the gym. Conversation was easy, and when he bent his head forward to kiss me on the stoop of the pub, I lent in closer, absorbing the warmth of his body and his sweet smell.

For our next date, he suggested we go to the Tracey Emin exhibition at White Cube. I was ten minutes late, and when I arrived he was leaning against the desk in the gift shop talking to the shop assistant, a copy of Emin's latest book in his hands. He smiled, indifferent to my lateness and excited to show me the paintings he liked most. It was his second visit to the gallery that week. With half an hour before closing, we didn't have long, so he pulled me along through the corridors of mini sketches to the giant red-splattered canvases that lined the next room.

Together, we stood in front of the exhibit's eponymous painting, *I Followed You to the End*, which showed a lone woman lying in bed – a black outline bathed in a crimson tempest as though drenched in blood. The lower half of the canvas was covered in a thick painted scrawl. 'You made me like this. All of you. You made me like this. I . . . was at fault to keep loving you, like a fool, I followed you to the end . . .'

I turned to Gym Boy and told him the painting made me angry because it made me think about all the men who hurt women. Who touch our bodies however they please, doing with them whatever they want and then walking off unscathed, unmoved while we are forever left with the imprint of their rough touch. Emin's body, like her paintings, is a cartography of scars – remembering sexual assault, abortion and the brutal legacy of the bladder cancer that almost killed her. She once described her experience of being raped at 13 as 'par for the course' for girls in her town (Margate). When a woman is depicted as crazy or unhinged or broken, I continued, we seldom hear about the men who made her that way, do we? He nodded in agreement. I wondered whether he too would leave me scarred.

I breathed in the anger Emin said fuelled much of her recent painting as I carried on walking around the gallery, looking for the thread of different endings as they were rendered on the canvas. I thought about the endings that characterised this period in my own life. I was in a space of transition.

Over the summer, Library Boy and I had made one final attempt at rekindling our romance. It had burned so bright so long ago that the warm embers continued, even now, to draw us back in. I was so in love with our story I couldn't let go of the possibility that we might still have our happy ending to write. And however cynical I had grown in the face of the romantic fantasy, there was a part of me that remained reluctantly enthralled to the idea that ours was a relationship defined by destiny. But meeting as adults, who were now strangers with a shared past, made for a complicated start to our romantic reunion. So while we tried to step back into an old and familiar intimacy, it seemed clear to us both that our story had finished. We had followed it to the very end.

I could also feel myself letting go of something else. I had been running the live event series Sex Talks for a while now, interviewing experts from across the sex and intimacy space, and had been struggling to delineate between my own personal exploration of intimacy and my journalistic engagement with a topic that had somehow become my life's work. I felt compelled to thrust myself into the story, if only to be able to report from the front lines that, yes, these were the conditions of the dating trenches from which I wrote, and, yes, said phenomenon was indeed a *very* real threat to connection. But I felt myself growing tired of loving and fucking for 'the plot'.

I no longer wanted to place my heart in a blender and my body on the line for the sake of writing another dating story scintillating enough to be worth retelling. I felt increasingly reluctant to offer up sore-hearted anecdotes to friends hungry for gossip as their children crawled beneath our feet, leaving chaos in their wake. I felt a relaxing of the death drive that had propelled me through my own chaos these past few years, and a burgeoning pull towards something calmer. In place of drama, I wanted peace. Besides, I could no longer bear to wake up next to a stranger, nor let someone I didn't know near my genitals (!). Remove the plot, and sex became for me something more than just fucking. Prude or whore, I no longer felt any emotional attachment to such labels – unconscious or otherwise. I just wanted to feel safe in the company of any person I slept alongside.

So when Gym Boy followed up after each date with a text saying it was nice to see me and asking when next I was free, I relished rather than recoiled from the apparent ease of our connection. I searched for the usual pangs of anxiety to reassure myself I fancied him. After all, love, or its simulacrum, had always arrived on a cloud of euphoria or deep anxiety. But instead what I found was a disorientating sense of calm. Odd.

Maybe I just liked that he texted me back. Or that when, in the early days, I said I didn't want to stay over after a date, despite being several drinks deep and already stretched out on his sofa, he said OK. And rather than interpret my no as a yes-in-waiting, a cue to tip-toe his hands towards my knickers until eventually I relented, instead he just pulled me close and kissed me. Like we were teenagers in a movie, high on the fumes of new romance. I liked that he seemed to feel entitled to neither my time nor my body, but enjoyed being around me as I enjoyed being around him. Or perhaps it was how he made me feel when we had sex: how his constant reassurance that I smelled and tasted so good finally convinced me I didn't need to shower every single time our bodies became entangled, but could instead relax into my nakedness while he worked his tongue across my flesh. Whatever residual shame still lingered beneath my skin began to ebb away with each encounter.

Soon, sex felt like our playground. A space for play rather than performance; for exploring new sensations rather than following a script I had learned but didn't enjoy. I bought us sex cards that depicted a variety of weird to wonderful new positions, which we tried out over several evenings, laughing as we contorted our bodies in novel ways. It all felt so deliciously primal. I didn't care that my body got sweaty, my hair became tangled, my makeup smudged. Because instead of watching us have sex from my usual external vantage point, I stayed in it. Present to his moans and my groans, telling him where I wanted to be touched and how. Moving his hand, his mouth, his body into exactly the place that felt best, while asking constantly what felt good for him. From our initial date we talked about sex – in the first instance around what I do, in the second what we both liked. And from there the conversation continued. An open dialogue that made sex feel easy. That was new.

So, one date turned quickly to two, which turned to three, until suddenly I was keeping a totally casual numbered list of every date we went on, if only to be able to report back to friends where on the scale of dating seriousness we were currently at.

But as we approached date number nine, I called him and said we needed to talk.

## Positive: Do I want to be a mother?

The Christmas parties were in full swing, and London was moving to the rhythm of an endless playlist of festive tunes. But something felt off. I'd been feeling strange for days – my body knotted and unusually tender, my emotions on a perpetual rollercoaster. I put it down to my impending period, all while sensing something was different. I did a pregnancy test just to put it out of my mind, and as I hurriedly got ready for a dinner I was already running 15 minutes late for, a bright blue cross appeared in the test window. The result you spend your sexually active adolescent life fearing and then your hopeful-parent years desperately holding out for.

Positive.

A wave of panic engulfed me. I did another test and, sure enough, the result was the same. The irony, I thought. Just that week I had been filming several ads for a condom campaign and, such were the endless edits this particular project required, I'd been saying into the camera virtually daily: 'Condoms are the most reliable way to avoid unwanted pregnancy.' You don't say.

Uncertain as to what to do or how to react, I shoved some lipstick and blush into my handbag and rushed to the Tube. When I arrived at the dinner, flushed and disorientated, I ran straight into a friend who squeezed me tight and asked, 'Babe, how are you?!'

'Great,' I responded. '*So* well.'

'No, babe, how are you really?' he replied earnestly.

*You don't want to know*, I thought. I ran to the toilet and cried.

The days that followed were a blur as I walked the halls of my old life feeling like a new woman I was not yet ready to become. It seemed odd to me that everyone I crossed paths with didn't automatically know a potential new life was brewing within me. How could something so huge for my body, so cataclysmic, be happening so quietly, unbeknownst to the rest of the world? I wanted to tell everyone. To shout from the rooftops, 'I'M PREGNANT!' Except that I didn't want to be pregnant at all.

I was 32 and surrounded by friends with babies, or else trying for babies, or else talking about babies. I thought maybe I'd have a baby someday too, although the prospect of endless sleepless nights and a schedule devoted to keeping another human alive was daunting. What had always felt inevitable, something that as a woman I had to do, had of late seemed less and less my predetermined destiny. The growing discourse around women opting to go child-free presented an appealing counter-narrative to motherhood essentialism, and while I could sort of imagine a future with children, I could just as happily imagine one without. At least, I thought I could.

I got home from dinner and looked at the two positive pregnancy tests, the bright blue crosses still visible on both screens, and tried to order my thoughts. To figure out where to begin. There was only one obvious course of action ahead of me, except something heavy tugged at the back of my mind. I knew I didn't want a baby right now, least of all with someone I had been on just eight dates with (although, who's counting?), but a whisper of what-ifs were now running through my head. *What if this is my only chance at having a baby? What if I'm not able to get pregnant again? What if it doesn't work out with Gym Boy and I never meet anyone else with whom to have a child?* My ambivalence towards motherhood was thrown suddenly into the lurch as I confronted a question I'd only ever had to entertain in the abstract: did I want to become a mother?

The Baader–Meinhof phenomenon refers to a cognitive bias whereby you notice or learn about something new – a word, idea or object – and then suddenly start seeing it everywhere. It's not that the thing is appearing more often, but that your brain has begun filtering information to prioritise what now feels relevant. It's often cited as the neuroscientific explanation for the power of manifesting: focus your attention on what you want in life and suddenly you will start seeing emblems of that thing everywhere. Now I was pregnant, babies were all I could think about. And suddenly, they were everywhere.

The following day, I waited for a call from the abortion clinic. When an unknown number popped up on my screen, I answered immediately, only to be met by a woman announcing she was calling from a fertility clinic and did I want to book in for a screening? It felt like a sick joke. I asked how she got my number, and she said I had registered interest in getting a fertility test on their website – that or a friend had done it for me. I resisted the urge to yell down the phone that I was pregnant and trying to speak to a doctor about an abortion, so *no*, I did not want a fertility test and nor did I want a reminder that my fertility was creeping closer towards a 'cliff edge'. Instead, I asked her to delete my details and hung up. My stomach clenched.

Finally, my phone buzzed again and it was the doctor. I explained my situation. A follow-up call was arranged. Then I put down the phone and opened a Word document on my laptop where I wrote: *15 August 2025*. I wanted to see it written down. I wanted to feel what it was like to see this date in front of me. Because if I kept the baby, this would be its due date. A real date on the calendar. A real point in time. It seemed incomprehensible to me that if I did nothing, if I said nothing, told no one and pretended this wasn't happening, then on that date my life would change profoundly. I closed my laptop and went for a walk. Then I texted Gym Boy, asking if we could meet the following evening at his. It was urgent.

I knew it wasn't his fault per se, but anger curdled in my stomach alongside the nausea. I decided that day that I hated him.

My diary entry read thus:


13 December, 2024

Today I feel rageful. Venomous. At him specifically and at mankind generally. Maybe God really is a man, a misogynist man at that, because biology is sexist as hell.


I am 32, single(ish) and pregnant, right before Christmas.


I'm angry that while my body is flooded with hormones, my tummy aching, my boobs sore, he is swanning about somewhere in the city, cracking on with life without a care in the world. I know I'm being unfair given that I have only just found out and haven't told him yet, but I resent that this is my secret to share, my burden to unload as I navigate through the admin involved in trying to sort this out. The very notion of 'sorting out' an unwanted pregnancy is in itself somewhat repellent. A woman's body too often relegated to a list of admin.


I went over to his house and, sitting at his kitchen table, I started with the admin: the calls I'd made, the appointments I'd booked, the dates I'd marked in my calendar. And then

I burst into tears. I want this so much, I told him through snot and tears, but not now. I couldn't do it right now. And nor, I knew, could he. He pulled me into his chest and repeated over and over again that everything was going to be OK.

I got up to go to the toilet and blow my nose, thinking about what a kind dad he'd be as I imagined this as our *Sliding Doors* moment. The point at which the course of my life would go one way, while I'd forever think regretfully about the other route it could have taken. My chest tightened. We had fast-forwarded from drinks and dinners and late-night, carefree sex, to contemplating becoming parents and discussing the practicalities of getting an abortion before Christmas. I had whiplash. When I returned to him on the sofa, I buried my head into the crook of his neck feeling pre-emptively bereft: for him, for a baby I didn't want but could suddenly imagine, for the relationship that was just getting started but would surely buckle under the weight of something so heavy, so early on. It was all so deeply unromantic. It was all so sad.

As I waited for my hospital appointment, I thought a lot about my body. It was a strange sort of limbo: existing as a pregnant person with all the hope, possibility and anxiety that implies, all while knowing that I wasn't going to have a baby. I have always found it difficult watching my body change. Being anorexic had given me a false sense of control over it, which I eventually had to relinquish in order to live. I tried thereafter to adopt a sense of ease with the changes that followed, but I often felt as though I was trapped in a stranger's body and my new skin didn't quite fit. More so when my body started to change more noticeably around my period. With every monthly fluctuation, I'd feel a creeping unfamiliarity with myself. Now, unintentionally pregnant, this mind–body dissonance was profound. My body didn't feel like my own.

A few nights before Gym Boy and I were expected at the hospital, I went to meet an old friend for lunch. She told me that she and her partner had been trying to get pregnant for several years and she was now on her third round of IVF. It was taking a big toll on her mental health. After multiple rounds of daily hormone injections accompanied by the assiduous monitoring of her follicle growth at endless doctors' appointments, they were making little progress. With every unsuccessful attempt at getting pregnant, her heart broke. The cycle of hope followed by disappointment was, she said, almost more agonising than the prospect of not being able to conceive. She wondered whether they would have to give up on their dream of having a baby biologically.

I felt a deep sense of shame.

It seemed so unjust that in that moment I had the very thing she and so many women want so terribly but cannot have, yet which I (ungratefully? irresponsibly? naively?) was opting out of. There was no guarantee that I would carry the baby to full term (one in eight pregnancies end in a miscarriage), but I wasn't even going to try. Was I making the wrong decision?

I held back tears as I hugged my friend tight and repeated the words Gym Boy had whispered in my ear just a few days before: everything is going to be OK. All while knowing that I couldn't promise her such a thing. She wanted to be a mother more than anything, and this was the route she had always anticipated taking to motherhood – the route every girl is made to believe she will one day, inevitably, follow. Now my friend was on the cusp of having to grieve a future upon which she had inadvertently hung so much of her self-worth as a woman, and on which her life plans had unconsciously become reliant.

Gym Boy and I sat in the waiting room together, listening for my name. I looked at the women around me, wondering what had brought each of them to this decision. Were they relieved to be sitting here? Were they resolute in their decision? Or was doubt lingering in the corners of their mind?

In 1964, French writer Annie Ernaux had an abortion at 23 years old. It was illegal at the time, so when her initial attempts to self-administer the procedure with a knitting needle failed, she elicited the help of an underground abortionist – known then as *faiseuse d'anges* or 'angel maker', a woman (typically not a doctor) who volunteered to terminate unwanted pregnancies. The clandestine abortion took place at the woman's apartment and resulted in a near-fatal haemorrhage which landed Ernaux in hospital. In an act of apparent generosity, the doctors there chose to label it a 'miscarriage' so Ernaux was spared prosecution – abortion was a crime punishable by imprisonment.

We know these details now because Ernaux wrote about the experience some 40 years later in her 2000 memoir *Happening* (*L'Evenement*), which set out to break the longstanding taboo around abortion. 'This thing had no place in language,' she wrote of the abortion, as she described herself poring over books in the library seeking solace in heroines who had gone through something similar. There were none to be found. Abortion was, she noted, catalogued exclusively among scientific or legal journals, which discussed the subject in the context of criminal justice. Although her own book was met with condemnation, since abortion was not considered a topic worthy of literary study, Ernaux was resolute. At the end of the book she wrote: 'I have finished putting into words what I consider to be an extreme human experience, bearing on life and death, time, law, ethics and taboo – an experience that sweeps through the body.'

Revisiting Ernaux's writing now, I am struck by the ways in which abortion has connected women over generations – like a thread that is woven through history: ever present, often barely visible. It is a point Betty Dodson notes in her foreword for *Cunt: A Declaration of Independence* (1998), as she observes how she and the book's author, Inga Muscio, both 'endured' abortions. But she is careful to note that in the time that elapsed between their respective procedures, great progress was made. 'One of mine was an illegal, kitchen-table abortion in the fifties, with a metal tool scraping out my uterus without any anesthesia,' she wrote. 'Inga's was, by contrast, "far more civilised."' I think about just how much of this progress is being undone in the US. How the clock has been turned back on the policing of women and their wombs.

One in three women will get an abortion at some point

in their lives. And, living in the UK, I was able to access the care I needed immediately. Within one day of finding out I was pregnant, I was on the phone to a nurse discussing my options and being talked through the next steps. In less than a week, I was taking the first tranche of pills I needed to proceed with a termination.

But in the background to my own decision, women just like me, women older and younger and far more vulnerable, women who had been raped, coerced, compelled into circumstances far worse than my own, were being denied the same right to make the biggest decision of their lives for themselves. History was again repeating itself.

Several days after I found out I was pregnant, South Carolina reintroduced a bill that would make abortion at any stage of pregnancy equivalent to murder under state law. By redefining 'person' under the state's criminal law to include a fertilised egg, anyone who obtained the procedure could potentially face the death penalty, or life in prison, for doing so. The brutality made me shudder. And while the bill was unlikely to pass into law, the sheer fact of its being proposed seriously by lawmakers bore testimony to how dramatically the pendulum had once again swung in America when it comes to abortion access.

Since the Supreme Court overruled *Roe v. Wade* in June 2022, 41 states across America have put abortion bans into effect,[51] with only limited exceptions. Twelve states have a total abortion ban, with South Carolina among the most aggressive in its restrictions. The architect of this particular bill originally introduced it in 2023, but the notion of lawmakers using capital punishment on people who get abortions sparked such outrage it went nowhere, and several Republicans who had co-sponsored the bill quickly removed their names. Now, emboldened no doubt by Trump returning to the White House, the reintroduced bill secured six co-sponsors. Naturally, they were all white men.

I would have been angered by the news story on any given day, but during that week it felt particularly personal. Visceral even. I tried to imagine how I would feel in my body if I were being forced to go through with the pregnancy, forced to watch my body change against my will, forced to plan for a life I didn't want and wasn't ready for. There seemed no greater cruelty than using such blunt political force to limit a woman's autonomy. To prioritise the rights of a cluster of cells, or a foetus, over and above a woman's life.

## Falling in love in the mundanity of the day-to-day

I sat in my living room, hunched over in pain as I filled giant nappy-sized pads with blood. I felt like an echo of Tracey Emin's bleeding woman. Except I wasn't alone.

I'm not sure when it happened, but at some point during my years of dating, I stopped asking for what I needed. I worked hard at being self-sufficient, priding myself on independence as I waxed lyrical about the power of building a life on my own terms. But perhaps somewhere along the line I confused independence for self-protection, erecting walls instead of boundaries. As I tried to play the cool girl who didn't care enough to get hurt, I continued to get hurt playing it cool. Then I got pregnant, and rather than feign insouciance in the face of Gym Boy's offers of support, I held out my hand and asked him to hold it. I couldn't do this on my own.

Did the days we spent then, curled up together on my sofa, watching box sets by the Christmas tree, count as dates? If so, we were racking them up fast. Ten, eleven, twelve. I finally believed him when he said it would be OK.

I thought of Ernaux and the fear she must have felt as she tracked down her backstreet abortion alone. Of the excruciating pain she would have endured just so she could try to maintain control over her own life. I thought of all the women throughout history who have sought, by any means, to terminate pregnancies they were not yet ready for, could not afford, or did not want. And I thought too of all the men who have got off scot-free. Who have never known the fear, the pain, the social stigma, or the shame that often accompanies a termination – termination, what a clinical word. I thought of all the men whose lives have been able to continue as they were because a woman they got accidentally pregnant 'sorted it out', taking full responsibility for an experience that ought always to be shared. I thought of Ernaux's solitude in her shame.

A week or so later, I went to my family home for Christmas, where the festive music was on full blast and the wine was flowing. I put on my favourite outfit, I wore my best shoes, and I applied bright red lipstick, all the while feeling I was only half there. I periodically went to the bathroom to change out another blood-soaked pad. Because of course you don't abort all in one go; you bleed for days, even weeks – a constant reminder of the fact that *yes* you were pregnant and *no* you are not pregnant anymore. It was both relief and pain all at once. Relief because I didn't want it, I wasn't ready for it and I knew that soon I'd be able to carry on with my life unchanged. What a privilege. Pain because I was plagued with the litany of questions that first shook my faith in the certainty of my decision.

How often must women perform normalcy while their bodies silently scream?

Christmas passed; I spent New Year's Eve in the countryside with some friends; and then the thrum of January began and life resumed. Time propelled forwards, carrying me with it, oblivious to the turning point that had crowned the end of the previous year in the form of my one tiny dot of life. Still, for a month or two, maybe three, I thought about the abortion a lot. I didn't feel sad or weighed down. I wasn't haunted by even a modicum of regret. I just found myself nudged daily into remembering those weeks in December.

I wondered how different the texture of my life would feel if I'd made a different decision – how I'd be thinking about the future. I imagined my tummy slowly swelling and felt awash with relief. The lack of any emerging bump was a reminder to me that I was free. Friends had suggested I do something ceremonial to commemorate the baby.

One had suggested a ritual of sorts while I was still in the process of bleeding, something involving candles and sage and nondescript chanting. But I didn't want to add layers of ceremony to the experience. Sometimes I wondered whether the absence of intense grief or even mild regret made me a bad woman, someone unworthy of ever becoming a mother. But I reminded myself I didn't owe anyone the performance of repentance, nor a justification wrapped in self-admonishment for a decision I knew was right for me. No woman needs to feel sad in order to feel justified for exercising her rights over her body.

Gym Boy checked in regularly to ask if I was still bleeding and in pain, but once the physical manifestation of The Thing had finished, thoughts of the abortion vanished too. One evening I asked him whether he thought about it at all, and he told me not really. I felt unsatisfied with his answer. I wanted him to think about it as much as I did. Or more. But I suppose for the person whose body is unaffected, the baby is always hypothetical and abstract. A proposition unfulfilled. I remembered an interview I'd done years ago with a nutritionist who specialised in baby loss. She'd told me that pregnancy hormones stay in your system for months after a termination, meaning it can take a while for your body to feel 'normal'. While my body was reminding me of what had happened, his was not.

Did he mull over what might have happened if I'd presented the situation to him differently? I pressed. As 'We're having a baby!' rather than, 'I'm pregnant and I want an abortion'?

He said he had considered it, and figured we'd just get on with it if that was the case. 'What else could we have done but make the best of it?' he responded. I felt comforted by his practicality. More so by his reassurance that he'd never imagined this as anything other than something we'd handle together, whatever the route we'd chosen. It was a trait of his I'd come to admire.

I returned thereafter to my research on sex and pleasure with a new lens, acutely aware that everything discussed in these pages is hollow if not accompanied by laws that protect a woman's right to bodily autonomy. What good is it to find your way back to a body that doesn't belong to you? To reclaim your connection to intimacy while living in the shadow of fear cast by brutal policymaking – designed to reinforce the most fundamental rupture between a woman and her body?

Pleasure requires the absence of pain. It also requires a basic sense of safety – a safety that anti-choice policies violently strip away. Because when women are robbed of the right to make decisions about our reproductive health, we are reduced to breeders. Our bodies are made mere vessels for an ideology that doesn't care if we live or die, and all in the name of the sanctity of life. The slogan 'Your body, my choice' comes to mind: a provocative subversion of the pro-choice epithet 'My body, my choice', which became a viral rallying cry for Trump supporters after his second election. The message then was clear: under the new administration, women's bodies would no longer be their own.

I have tried to imagine what it might be like to have sex

with a man in an area of the world where abortions are banned. To summon the sense of blissful abandon that orgasm-inducing sex often requires, all while a niggling thought at the back of my head reminds me: condoms break and contraception fails, you could get pregnant and then . . . The very real possibility of sex leading to death was not exactly what Georges Bataille meant by *la petite mort.* And so I cannot envisage a joyful pursuit of pleasure under conditions in which my body is a place beyond my jurisdiction. How could any woman?

## His favourite fruit is a persimmon

The day before I had the abortion, I had a session with an astrologer, Noura Bourni. I didn't want to tell her the specifics of why I was so insistent we speak on this particular day and no other, but instead asked her to paint a picture of what the forthcoming year would hold for me. I'm sure I craved some cosmological reassurance that I was making the right choice, but I was also curious to know whether the stars might in fact be aligned for me and Gym Boy. I was worried the abortion would be our last Great Act and needed a second opinion. She made a note of our respective birthdays and examined her charts. We were well aligned, she said. This was something that could really last. I looked at her sceptically. 'Why not?' she responded. I sat back and thought about it.

During the weeks that followed, Noura's words danced in the back of my mind as Gym Boy and I moved past our weeks of hospital-shaped romance into a new stage of dating. I kept updating my list. Date #14: Boxing Day movie and dinner. Date #15: Gallery visit followed by burgers. Date #16: Cook together. I got all the way up to Date #19: Christmas tree take-down and dinner, before I apparently lost interest in meticulously documenting our budding romance. By then he'd bought me a toothbrush for his bathroom and given me keys to his flat – a strong indication, said a committee of friends, that he was not a fuck boi planning on jumping ship without warning, and this was not a situationship. I remained cautious.

But weeks quickly turned to months, until one day we were sitting at his kitchen table over a long weekend, me working on my book and he finishing a deck for his new business, when a familiar feeling began to course through my body.

'I'm going to start cooking us lunch,' he said, bending over to kiss me. 'This is so fun isn't it?'

'What, working on a bank holiday?' I laughed.

'Being productive and cosy together.'

I got up and followed him to the counter as he started cutting up vegetables for my favourite salad, tossing everything into a giant mustard-coloured bowl while humming something indistinguishable. I wrapped my arms around his waist from behind, resting my head on his back.

A passage from Gabrielle Zevin's *Tomorrow and Tomorrow and Tomorrow* (2022) surfaced in my mind. When Marx and Sadie move into their first home together as a couple, Marx wanders into the garden and plucks a persimmon from their tree, delighted. How lucky are we, he exclaims, to have bought a house with a tree that bears my favourite fruit. Sadie looks at him holding his juicy treasure, wondering whether she has ever heard him so much as mention a persimmon before. Was it really his favourite fruit? It was then that she realised: the 'luck' constantly attributed to Marx by friends, in life, in love and in business, was a different kind of good fortune. One born from his unique propensity to see everything through the lens of 'fortuitous bounty'. My God, she thinks, 'he is so easy to love'.

I buried my face into Gym Boy's neck. *God*, I thought, *you are so easy to love.*

For years I'd searched for connection in pockets of romantic highs, mistaking anxiety for excitement; fixation for desire; and intensity for intimacy. Love, I thought, was fought for on a battlefield – we all bear the scars to prove it. But this? This felt easy. No armour required. I realised then, standing in his kitchen, that I'd fallen in love for the second time, in neither a high nor a low, but, simply, in the mundanity of the day-to-day.

'Hee-Won,' I said, pulling him closer. 'Can we go away together?'

He turned around, smiling. 'Of course. I'd love that.'


## 15 August

There is no such thing as the perfect novel, author Coco Mellors said to me in an interview once, but if there was, it would be James Baldwin's *Giovanni's Room* (1956). I bought it the following day and have returned to it often since, my fingers thumbing through the pages impatiently each time to find one particular quote. 'Nothing is more unbearable, once one has it,' Baldwin writes, 'than freedom. I suppose this is why I asked her to marry me, to give me something to be moored to. Perhaps this was why . . . she decided that she wanted to marry me. But people can't unhappily invent their mooring posts, their lovers and their friends, any more than they can invent their parents. Life gives these and also takes them away, and the great difficulty is to say "Yes" to life.'

I returned to *Giovanni's Room* over the summer, reaching for a familiar story amid another great life shift.

I packed up my flat and put my life into boxes for the tenth time in just as many years, and thought about all the people alongside whom I've tried to moor myself in vain. All the men I have dated in the hopes that they might rescue me from the uncertainty and indecision of my own freedom. That they might anchor me in some sense of self that I couldn't for a time seem to find alone. I hoped that one of them, any of them, might offer up some answers. It's what I wanted from my first great love and it's what I instinctively and unconsciously expected from everyone who came after him, as I went out in search of that Platonian other half, all the while building avatars in my head out of potential lovers on a screen. I wanted them all to love me not so that I could love myself (how cliché), but so that I could get to know myself: through their eyes; from their perspective.

I no longer want anyone to tell me who I am, I thought as

I filled another box. But I do like the idea of relationships as mooring posts. More so the notion that the challenge is not to set out in search of buoys upon which to cling. But instead to say yes to life while moving along with the current, calm in the knowledge that buoys will come and they will go. The only consistent mooring is oneself. That had always seemed to me quite a depressing thought, but now it felt freeing.

I got on my bike and cycled to the Post Office in search of more tape. It was a clear, blue-skied day and the streets were bathed in sunshine – even We Buy Any Porn, with its blacked-out windows, was illuminated in the early-morning glow. I pedalled along, making a mental checklist of everything I still had to pack, and considered what Baldwin said about freedom and it feeling like an unbearable weight once one has it. I disagreed. Over the past eight months or so, I'd stepped back into my life with renewed vigour. Newly appreciative of my freedom as a woman without a child. In another time or another place, I would not have had this freedom, nor the bodily autonomy that is its prerequisite. Nothing could be more unbearable than that.

I booked a Zipcar and drove some of my boxes to Hee-Won's house. He was waiting outside for me when I arrived and started unloading the boot while I pulled out various lamps from the back seat, lining them up on the pavement in order of size. He laughed and walked over to the front door with several boxes in his arms, ushering me to follow him into our home.

We spent the rest of the day unpacking, and by the time

I had crushed the final cardboard box beneath my feet, my body was wilting with fatigue. I collapsed onto the sofa and rested my head on his shoulder as we observed our shared surroundings. My things were spilling out from every cupboard and drawer, bringing a new layer of chaos to his otherwise calm home. The doorbell rang and I got up to let Elspeth in. She was carrying a giant bouquet of multicoloured flowers and champagne to celebrate the big move.

We sat at the table, and I poured three glasses so we could toast to new beginnings.

'Do you know what day it is today?' I said to them both.

'What is it?' Elspeth responded.

'It's August 15th.'

## Chapter 11

# In pursuit of pleasure for pleasure's sake

I read recently that writing a memoir requires peeling back the presentable layers of the self, those that tell the story we want the world to know about us. Insofar as we tell ourselves stories in order to live, the writer of memoir must unpack the stories that help her survive, in order to expose the truth upon which such necessary fabrications are built. Only then can we begin to find our way back to ourselves. And only then can we speak honestly about who we are, and what made us this way.

I often think about the woman who sat in her bedroom divulging the contents of her sex life to a therapist in Australia. I think about the stories that shaped the way she saw the world and her place in it. And I think about how different her life would have been if she'd never admitted to a group of women at a dinner party that she couldn't orgasm.

I told myself I was broken because, for a time, it was easier to see myself as unfixable than to unpack the stories I thought explained why. I held my twin pillars of shame – an eating disorder and sexual disconnect – close. They were the dirty little secrets I lugged around for much of my life, all the while convincing myself I was unaffected by their double burden. That it mattered little how I related to my body, because my body didn't matter. The stories we tell ourselves in order to live. But as Carl Jung wrote, 'One does not become enlightened by imagining figures of light, but by making the darkness conscious.'[52] I had to reconcile with these shadow parts of myself in order to make peace with my body, and I had to make peace with my body in order to experience pleasure. It's hard to feel joy in a body you've learned to hate. Harder still to show up fully in the world while embroiled in a war against yourself.

In bringing these hidden parts of myself to the fore, in the therapy room and then in the countless conversations and interviews that followed, and now in the pages of this book, I stepped out from the darkness in which shame thrives and into a dialogue I realised so many women were already a part of. The story sustains you until you realise there's a better one. And for me that better one had been written over and over again across centuries.

Women have been disconnected from their bodies throughout history, victim to a patriarchal culture that teaches us to perform our desirability for the enjoyment of men; to forgo our own pleasure in service of others; to stay strangers to our bodies, to fear them as they age; to understand our worth in terms of our fuckability and impregnatability. What stories. But wherever you find evidence of this project of disconnection, you find women pushing back. Women who have cultivated a deeper knowledge of their bodies and discovered what Audre Lorde referred to as the spiritual, creative plane within the feminine that is the erotic.

I interviewed one such woman a year or so ago. Her name is Regena Thomashauer, and she's the founder of the School of Womanly Arts and author of *Pussy: A Reclamation*. During our conversation, she explained the difference she sees in a woman once she has connected to her sensuality. There is a clear before and after, she said. In the 'before', she is at odds with her body. She doesn't understand it. Her lights are switched off. Then she discovers her pleasure and everything changes. 'It's like learning how to put your key in your own ignition – turn that baby on, take her down the highway.

'When you start being clitorate, when you start knowing your body, when you have really done the research on yourself, then you can teach a partner what you like.'

I have thought about that image many times since we spoke. Often when in conversation with other women as they've described to me their own journeys of sexual self-discovery, or as one woman phrased it, her 'Second Coming'. We were sitting next to one another at a work dinner and quickly the conversation turned to sex. She was from America and had grown up in a Mormon community, she explained, abstaining from sex until marriage and then dutifully enduring a marriage with little sex and no intimacy. They were together for 15 years, she told me, until one day she snapped. Her body wanted more than perfunctory touch, and she wanted more than love with no desire. She asked for a divorce and has since been exploring her connection to sexuality for the first time. Her life, she said, had been thrust into Technicolor. I nodded in agreement; so had mine.

The word 'Technicolor' played through my head that night as I walked home. It felt so apt a description of my own evolution over the past few years as my world had become drenched in new colour. The change had been gradual, rather than akin to a post-orgasm high, and underpinned by the new lens through which I'd learned to see my body – through the prism of pleasure rather than pain and punishment. In undergoing sex therapy I had ended a 17-year cycle with bulimia and changed the way I walked through the world. The way I moved in my body. How I showed up during intimacy. And while sex had always been something I'd dreaded, something couched in anxiety and body shame, now I saw it very differently. It was a space for play and exploration rather than performance; somewhere I sought to be curious rather than restricted by a script I'd learned but didn't enjoy. Sex, I'd discovered, felt best when it was animalistic and silly rather than serious; exploratory as opposed to prescriptive. (To this end I only half-jokingly declared 2025 my Year of Anal. All in the name of research.)

Someone said to me in an interview once that developing

confidence in the bedroom bolsters your confidence in the boardroom, which I undoubtedly think is true. When you learn to advocate for your needs and establish your boundaries in the most intimate part of your life, it has a ripple effect on how you show up elsewhere.

I have come to think of the stories women share among ourselves regarding bodies and pleasure as the ones that truly bind us. Connecting a long lineage of women who have at some point refused to perform the pseudo-eroticism foisted upon them by a society that wants to reduce us to empty 'sex symbols'. Women who have then set out in search of something more, while bringing others along with them. Teaching women how to masturbate *à la* Betty Dodson; educating women about their bodies like the Boston Women's Collective; sharing their learnings from the *Kama Sutra* like Seema Anand; reimagining what porn could be, like Erika Lust and Cindy Gallop; distinguishing a performed sexuality from the truly erotic like Audre Lorde. In the face of rupture, these women sought reconnection.

And so I find myself thinking back constantly to a group of women from many centuries ago, whose story I discovered by accident while looking for another book in the London Library. Translated from French, *The Distaff Gospels* describes a group of peasant women in 15th-century France who gathered regularly to spin flax and talk about men, marriage, pregnancy and family life. During one of these meetings they decided that their collective wisdom must be preserved for all the women that would come after them (women were largely excluded from mainstream medical discourse at the time, so relied almost entirely on communal, oral knowledge about childbirth, fertility and the body). Most peasant women were illiterate, so they appointed an obnoxious-sounding neighbour, who likened himself to a divine chronicler, as their scribe. Over the weeks that followed, they dictated more than 200 pieces of advice to him: on marriage, desire, childbirth, the anxieties of young women, and of course the eternally important question of how to secure a man's affections. One woman claimed that feeding a man catnip would ensure his undying devotion. I have yet to try it.

Setting aside the suspect nature of their advice, the significance of this story has stayed with me. Specifically, the image of a group of women many centuries ago passing on the very body knowledge they had no formal recourse to. Such informal networks of knowledge exchange have been essential to how women have learned about their bodies and their sensuality. I now imagine Sex Talks through this same lens. And I have also embarked on a new venture in this vein. I am now studying to become a qualified sex and relationship coach, on a course that focuses on somatic practices designed to deepen connection and intimacy, all while integrating insights from neuroscience, attachment theory, and emotional intelligence. In the spirit of the Distaff women, I hope to continue passing on the body knowledge that was handed to me in the sex therapy room, and which I now know to be transformative.

Growing up, we're handed a Disney-informed version

of love that says our goal as women is to find our Prince Charming and let the fairy tale begin. Putting aside the perils of such heteronormative romantic essentialism, which says our happiness depends on finding a half to make us whole, this mythology of love suggests the only real challenge is finding our person. The 'what next' is a footnote apparently unworthy of investigation. But just as we must learn what it takes to cultivate love daily, beyond the falling and in the mundanity of the day-to-day, our connection to pleasure requires similar nurturing. A rewilding of our gardens and a tending to new plants. A reclamation of our bodies in pursuit of pleasure for pleasure's sake.

# Acknowledgements

Firstly, this book would never have come into fruition without my incredible literary agent, Abigail Bergstrom. She believed in what this book could be even before I did, and has helped shape my words and my thinking ever since. I love working with you!

Secondly, my brilliant book editor, Carole Tonkinson. Carole's instincts as to where this book should go have pushed me to write the best piece of work I could, and I feel so lucky to have been able to write something so personal in such safe and talented hands.

And then of course I want to acknowledge the team at Bonnier and at LEAP. It takes a village to publish a book and theirs is a powerful one. Particular thanks to: Arabella, Tamara, Saira and Emily.

Of course I must thank my sex therapist, Aleks Trkulja, whose tender and thoughtful insights in the sex therapy room profoundly changed my life for the better. None of this would have happened were it not for your brilliant mind and extraordinary skills as a therapist.

Sharmadean Reid who commissioned me to write the series *Conversations With My Sex Therapist for The Stack World*. I love a business incentive and doubt whether I would ever have taken the plunge to do sex therapy had it not been for the lure of writing about it (I'm an exhibitionist like that). Sharmadean is the purveyor of excellent ideas and I feel lucky to have been able to run with one of her (in my eyes, naturally) best.

I want to also thank the incredible Aimee Phillips who first commissioned the event series at its OG home: The Edition Hotel. "What do you need to make it happen?" she asked me. Then rustled up everything we required to get started. We love the hustle of a New Yorker. And of course, Caroline Lever, who returned from mat leave as excited for these conversations as I was. She was an incredible champion for the series and imbued her great taste in helping shape future programming.

Sitting front row at virtually every Sex Talks event I've ever hosted is my best friend Elspeth Merry. She is the sort of friend you read about in books but seldom believe could exist in real life: fiercely loyal; unendingly thoughtful and always up for an adventure. I hope we get to laugh together forever. Where would we be without our Earth-Angel, Rob H? The glue that holds together the long-haired trio; the person who makes me feel ten times more gorgeous and entirely unstoppable. I adore you!

My sister, Lucy Boynton, who has held me through everything, for quite literally her entire life. She is the wisest person I know and offers the most reassuring and calming advice to any and all situations. We don't get to pick our family, but I would pick you a thousand times over to be my best-sister-friend, Lucy B. I cannot imagine life without you.

But Lucy is the way she is because we have enviably wonderful parents. The sort of parents you grow up shouting at when you're an insolent and insufferable teen, then go onto revere the older you get. My mum, Adriaane, is both my and my sister's life support. The person we call daily, often multiple times, and upon whom we remain as reliant today (in our thirties no less) as we were as children. Her capacity for kindness and care knows no bounds. It's a privilege to know unconditional love, and that is what she gives our entire family.

My dad, Graham, for constant support and, dare I say it, entertainment. He is the person I have looked up to my entire life, not just because of his writing accomplishments, but because of his relentless worth ethic, which sees no sign of waning. He is the hardest working person I know, and also the most supportive. I am my father's daughter and there could be no higher praise.

I couldn't have asked for better parents, I love you both more than you know.

Hee-Won: we fell in love in the mundanity of the day-to-day, but our love is anything but mundane. It is the sort of expansive, life-affirming love that I wasn't sure I'd ever find.

I feel inordinately lucky to be on your team because life is just so much better by your side. I'm so glad we found each other.

And finally I want to thank all my friends who have been so supportive and kind throughout this entire writing process: Olivia P for being such a constantly kind and supportive friend; Alya M and Ellie H, whose writing advice was invaluable. Claire B and Sharmadean R for the best chats and moral support. My first Great Love, LHW. You taught me how to love and how to be loved in return, and I will forever cherish our years together. Thank you for your blessing in reflecting on that love in this book.

Roxie N for her unending support, her words of wisdom and for just being the kindest champion to those around her. Gabby C for pushing me to write this book before I believed it was even possible, and for being the best cheerleader there was throughout. Giles W and Arthur K, my forever dinner dates, however fast our lives may suddenly be changing. Berry P de C for being the most incredible AP on Sex Talks. Rachel C, Bella S and Sasha S for being my Manchester OGs and putting up with my long periods of being MIA while in the library. Sep B for, just, everything. Ryan A for holding me down in the heady spin of my NYC days. Lauren M, Amy F, Al G for being the dream team, always. Sophie H for having the same brain as me and cheering me on along the way. Christina D who read the entire manuscript before it went to proof and whose thoughtful and kind reflections reminded me why these conversations are so important.

# Endnotes

## Introduction

1    https://bloodknife.com/everyone-beautiful-no-one-horny/

2    Institute of Practitioners in Advertising study - https://ipa.co.uk/news/touchpoints-2025

3    https://www.demandsage.com/screen-time-statistics/

4    https://www.bmj.com/content/365/bmj.l1525

5    https://healf.com/blogs/health-journal/biohack-your-sex-life

6    https://www.standard.co.uk/lifestyle/bryan-johnson-longevity-controversial-tips-b1217229.html

7    https://blueprint.bryanjohnson.com/blogs/news/how-i-m-de-aging-my-penis?srsltid=AfmBOopKjyMHPB1iH_fzYvpINS-XqLapv12KjNhD-K7aQlvcKEXnoZQak

8    https://pubmed.ncbi.nlm.nih.gov/17610060/#:~:text=Abstract,Love%20and%20Commitment%20and%20Expression.

## Chapter 2

9    https://www.gcimagazine.com/brands-products/news/news/22068577/report-almost-23-of-executives-in-beauty-industry-are-men

10   https://faculty.uml.edu/kluis/42.101/Bartky_FoucaultFeminityandthe-Modernization.pdf

11   https://creoclinic.com/blog/brazilian-butt-lift-statistics/

12   https://www.plasticsurgery.org/news/press-releases/plastic-surgery-societies-issue-urgent-warning-about-the-risks-associated-with-brazilian-butt-lifts

13   https://pmc.ncbi.nlm.nih.gov/articles/PMC4438277/

14   https://pubmed.ncbi.nlm.nih.gov/18056239/

15   Brown TM. Alfred C. Kinsey: A Pioneer Of Sex Research. American Journal of Public Health (2003)

16   https://www.nytimes.com/2001/02/19/us/william-h-masters-a-pioneer-in-studying-and-demystifying-sex-dies-at-85.html

17   https://www.nice.org.uk/guidance/qs175/documents/briefing-paper

18   Frederick, D. A., St. John, H. K., Garcia, J. R., & Lloyd, E. A. (2018). Differences in Orgasm Frequency Among Gay, Lesbian, Bisexual, and Heterosexual Men and Women in a U.S. National Sample. Archives of Sexual Behavior. 47(1): 273–288

19   Personal communication with Dr Karen Gurney (date), referring to her The truth about faking orgasms TED Talk; specific figure not available in publicly accessible transcript.

**Chapter 3**

20   https://www.forbes.com/sites/allysonkapin/2023/12/14/dear-big-tech-and-vc-yet-again-youve-failed-women/

21   https://compostingfeminisms.wordpress.com/wp-content/uploads/2020/04/andrea-dworkin-renouncing-equality.pdf

22   https://lareviewofbooks.org/article/the-ideology-of-masturbation/

**Chapter 4**

23   https://www.dodsonandross.com/articles/women-having-independent-orgasms-will-change-world

24   https://www.dodsonandross.com/articles/women-having-independent-orgasms-will-change-world

25   Chapter One, Sex For One

26   https://lareviewofbooks.org/article/the-ideology-of-masturbation/

27   https://medium.com/@fitmind.app/visualise-your-way-to-success-cacb6450498c

28   https://pmc.ncbi.nlm.nih.gov/articles/PMC2857771/

29   Chapter one

30   Brown, Brené. *I Thought It Was Just Me (but it isn't): Women Reclaiming Power and Courage in a Culture of Shame*. Gotham Books, 2007.


**Chapter 5**

31   https://warwick.ac.uk/fac/cross_fac/iatl/research/reinvention/archive/volume6issue1/oleary/

32   https://library.oapen.org/handle/20.500.12657/35002

33   Levack, Brian P. The Witch-Hunt in Early Modern Europe. 3rd ed., London: Routledge, 2006, pp. 21–26, 203–208.

34   Silvia Federici, Caliban and the Witch: Women, the Body and Primitive Accumulation (Autonomedia, 2004).

35   https://stephenfollows.com/p/are-men-in-romantic-films-older-than-women

36   https://gen-m.com/wp-content/uploads/2021/09/GenM-Invisibility-Report.pdf

37   https://www.mordorintelligence.com/industry-reports/anti-aging-products-market

38   Nir Eyal, Hooked: How to Build Habit-Forming Products (New York: Portfolio/Penguin, 2014), Introduction.other


**Chapter 7**

39   https://www.nytimes.com/2012/05/20/fashion/weddings/how-the-vows-column-came-about.html

40   https://www.youtube.com/watch?v=kan2ZGqEOso

41   https://longreads.com/2014/02/20/swiping-right-in-the-1700s-the-evolution-of-personal-ads/

42   https://longevity.stanford.edu/the-tyranny-of-choice/

43   Gabor Maté, In the Realm of Hungry Ghosts: Close Encounters with Addiction (Knopf Canada, 2009)

44   https://www.youtube.com/watch?v=NrF91EOuSKQ


**Chapter 8**

45   https://www.reddit.com/r/replika/comments/118oo6m/my_wife_is_dead/

46   https://x.com/simonsinek/status/963782657246195712?lang=en&utm


**Chapter 9**

47   https://pubmed.ncbi.nlm.nih.gov/32661813/

48   https://www.childrenscommissioner.gov.uk/resource/sex-is-kind-of-broken-now-children-and-pornography/

49   https://juliebindel.substack.com/p/why-andrea-dworkin-is-the-radical-4ad

50   https://www.lrb.co.uk/the-paper/v09/n12/roy-porter/signor-cock?utm_source=chatgpt.com


**Chapter 10**

51   https://www.guttmacher.org/state-policy/explore/state-policies-abortion-bans#:~:text=shortly%20after%20birth.-,Highlights,bans%20based%20on%20gestational%20duration.

52   C.G. Jung, Psychology and Alchemy, trans. R.F.C. Hull, Collected Works of C.G. Jung, Vol. 12 (Princeton: Princeton University Press, 1968), para. 335.